T0150953

# Advance Praise

"Davis paves a fantastic path from heavy healing to really living some much-needed lightheartedness!"

—**Christy Ann Clark**, CoHost of the podcast
*Perceptionists Anonymous*

"If you're a gamer or just a human being on a stealth mission to find the perfect solution for your relationship anxiety, I have seven words for you: It's dangerous to go alone. Take this..."

—**Kristalynn Vetovich**, Bestselling Author of
*Driven Fearless*

# Damsel No More!

# Damsel N⦶ MORE

The Secret to
Slaying Your Anxiety
& LOVING AGAIN
After an Abusive
Relationship

# Emily Davis

NEW YORK

LONDON • NASHVILLE • MELBOURNE • VANCOUVER

# Damsel No More!

## The Secret to Slaying Your Anxiety and Loving Again After an Abusive Relationship

Published in New York, New York, by Morgan James Publishing. Morgan James is a trademark of Morgan James, LLC. www.MorganJamesPublishing.com

ISBN 9781642799194 paperback
ISBN 9781642799200 eBook
Library of Congress Control Number: 2019956004

**Cover Design by:**
Rachel Lopez
www.r2cdesign.com

**Interior Design by:**
Christopher Kirk
www.GFSstudio.com

Morgan James is a proud partner of Habitat for Humanity Peninsula and Greater Williamsburg. Partners in building since 2006.

Get involved today! Visit
MorganJamesPublishing.com/giving-back

*For my parents; there will never be enough ways to thank you.*

# Table of Contents

# Acknowledgments

Thank you to Angela Lauria and The Author Incubator's team, as well as to David Hancock and the Morgan James Publishing team for helping me bring this book to print. To say this is a dream come true doesn't even begin to describe it.

# Why Your Anxiety Is Ruining Your Relationship

**Y**ou are strong. I know, kind of an odd statement to start a book about overcoming anxiety, but stay with me on this one. You are strong. You have overcome so much just to be sitting here reading this. You left your abusive ex even though it was hard – like, harder than hard – and you are determined never to end up in a relationship like that ever again.

So, you took time for yourself. You took time to remember who you were again without the attachment of a relationship.

You learned to be free again. You learned who you were again. And it felt amazing. You healed, and you laughed, and you went out when you wanted and ate what you wanted. You didn't have to please anyone else, and for perhaps the first time, you truly understood the beauty in that feeling.

For a while, you waited; you didn't want another relationship. Not necessarily because you were afraid of love or even that you were afraid of giving your power up to someone else again, but because you wanted to have some time to rediscover you. Also, you didn't want to go back to that mind-set. You know the one. The mind-set where you must please your partner at all costs, where you feel like you require their approval to exist, where you are somehow in their debt because they are with you. Screw that. You wanted to make sure that the next relationship was a good one, where you were ready, where you were strong.

Then you met him, that sweet, funny man who you can tell genuinely likes you for you. Not only that, he likes everything you do. He is kind and cares about you, and every time you are with him, you feel like the sky is the limit. I bet you two can spend hours playing games or watching cartoons. And so you thought, *Ok, it must be time.*

First of all, that step alone takes a ton of strength and growth to be so brave, to accept someone back into your life again. But now you are a few months in (or perhaps even a year in), and you can't stop the anxiety that keeps creeping up on you. It's getting bad. You keep slipping back into that pattern of fear. Fear that you will make him unhappy. Fear that you won't be enough for him. Fear that he will leave you because you keep vomiting your anxiety out all over him.

And the doubt. You doubt yourself; you thought you had done the healing, done the work to be better. But then why is this happening? You are a strong person, you left, so why do you still feel so much like a victim? And your current boyfriend is so kind and caring, how come you can't just accept his love?

Are you the problem? You wonder more and more. Are you just bad at relationships? And, the worst doubt of all, the one that you don't even want to say out loud not even to yourself – am I the reason my last relationship turned abusive? Am I the unhealthy one?

That thought is scary, and I know it can feel so daunting.

The problem with healing from abuse (or any trauma for that matter) is that you don't know how deeply you are hurt until you are back in the situation that caused the hurt. So, with abusive relationships in particular, when you are back in a relationship is the time that so much of the pain you went through will bubble to the surface.

If you are anything like most of my clients, you probably lead a really busy life. You have a successful career that you have built for yourself. You don't have time to go to therapy, and you also don't have time to sit in a relationship where you feel like you are spinning in circles. And your current partner is so wonderful you don't want to lose him, but, seriously, you just want to be in a healthy relationship. To have the kind of love that you can count on.

Mostly, you are tired of being afraid – so, so tired. You're afraid that you will lose your relationship, or worse, that your partner will resent you for having this anxiety and grow bitter toward you for not being able to stop the fear from destroying everything. But you still stay because he genuinely cares about you.

You are also afraid of being cared about. You didn't think you would be because that is what you have always wanted in a partner, but having someone take care of you freaks you the heck out. You are afraid that you will owe them something, and don't even get me started on your fears in the bedroom.

But, as I have stated, you are strong. And you are not going to let your fear hold you back from having the relationship and life that you deserve. I know you want a healthy relationship. You want someone you can count on to be there for you when you need them to be. You want to have someone to go with you to the party.

I have been there. Right there in the same shoes that you are in now. I know it feels like if you don't do something to stop your anxiety, you may never have a healthy relationship, a fulfilling relationship, and that you will lose the partner you care so much about.

This is what I like to call your Heck Freaking No Moment.

This is the turning point where you conquer your fears for good, where you slay all the pain that your ex put you through. It's where you stop having to live through the anxiety that you still carry with you from that jerk. You have given him enough time. You have given him enough of your life.

You are done paying the price for someone else's bad choices with your happiness.

In this book and with this method, you will learn how to slay your fears for good through play. Yup, you heard me, you have spent way too freaking long living in seriousness. Its time you use your light to overcome. It's time for you to have some fun and build a relationship that is as strong as you, the relationship that you have always dreamed of, one that is fun and full of communication and caring.

This may be hard to fully imagine at the moment, but just remember, you are here. You have made it so far and been through so much. Now is your time to kick your demons in the face.

# I Promise It's Not Just You

ow, before we dive in, I want to tell you a bit about my journey.

When I was sixteen I met the "most amazing guy." Psych – dude was a butthole. But I sure as heck didn't know it, and I defended him tooth and nail against any nay-sayers (i.e., my parents and friends who genuinely cared about my well-being). After high school, he moved away with me for college. That is when things got serious…and seriously bad.

I had my son at the end of November of my first semester of college. He was premature, and I was terrified. I made the choice to leave school and started working full-time in a call center, far from the awesome career in archeology that I had always dreamed about. To quell that pain, I threw all my effort into my relationship. He was my world.

We married the weekend before my nineteenth birthday, and that is when the switch really happened. It was as if my "awesome boyfriend" had been pretending to be awesome the whole time we were dating, but now that we were married, he didn't have to try anymore. Huh, imagine that. He viewed me as a possession at that point, and I was stuck. Like really, really badly stuck.

He was the typical abuser, sociopath, and pathological liar; he abused me in every way possible, and that eventually spread to my children. Soon, he got afraid that my parents would convince me to leave him, so he told me that we needed to move to get away from my family. So we did.

As with most people in an abusive relationship, I was completely brainwashed into the "I deserve it, he still loves me, I owe him for tolerating me" cycle.

There are two distinct moments that I first remember thinking that something was wrong, and that I was actually being abused.

The first was when I had gone into work the day after he had beat the crap out of me with his car keys. I was cut and deeply bruised on every part of my body except my face, and that morning he had looked at me as I left and said, "I didn't hurt you; I never touched your face. You can't tell me that's abuse." And when I went into work, I casually tried to show my boss some of the bruising, laughing and giving a garbage excuse of a skateboarding accident. He laughed and called me clumsy. And I thought, you know, maybe the fact that I am trying to get my boss to help me (I was selling cars at the time and he was a sleezy fella) means that I actually do need some help.

The second time was when we had moved from a small house to an apartment after being evicted (I had also just been fired for the first and only time in my entire life). He was yelling at me about how it was all my fault and how he hated the move. I was sobbing and someone knocked on the door. It was our new neighbor, and she looked at my tear-stained face and asked if I was okay. I nodded. And she asked if I needed her to call someone. I shook my head no and closed the door. That night, I wondered why I hadn't asked her to call the police. It was the first time I wondered why I was protecting him.

I left him not too long after that. He spent some time in jail and I got a series of very tight restraining orders and custody agreements.

And then I did *everything*.

I took my kids outside and to the park and they went to preschool and playdates. All things he never would let them do.

And I got my own place in my hometown and got a job doing the one thing that I had always loved: horseback riding.

I became a horseback trail guide in the Lake Tahoe mountains, and it was one of the best experiences of my life. I connected with my authentic self again, a person that I hadn't seen in years. I let her come out, and she found her power again through bucking hay and avoiding bears. I understood what it felt like to learn again and lead again, and I started to heal. It felt so good to be free.

But that amazing gig was seasonal, summers only, so I had to find a winter plan. I fell into a ski resort's human resources position. At first, that was only winters, but I moved up, and then up again within the same year, and then another time. This was the next stage of healing for me, the reminder that I could achieve again, that I was successful, that I could be whatever and do whatever I wanted, and that nothing could hold me back.

With each passing day, my ex was fading further and further into the past. And I was feeling more and more healed. But I did have a nagging worry; I was concerned about letting anyone into my life again. I wanted to protect my kids, and I wanted to protect myself. I didn't know how I would be with someone. Abusive was all I had known a relationship to be. I didn't want to have my unseen problems become someone else's.

I took my time. I was cautious. And then the perfect man for me fell right into my lap. He was kind and a single dad. He had a little girl who was a year older than my son and two years older than my daughter. He was nerdy; he was into anime and books and Ren faires. He wanted to know about me, about what I liked so he could be involved in what made me smile, and he was interested in who I was as a person. Things were comfortable with him. Safer than I ever could have imagined.

I remember during the beginning of our relationship, I expressed my fears to him. I didn't know how I was going to act, I didn't know what would trigger me, and I was worried how that would end up reflecting on me. He took this warning in stride and stated that he fully supported me in whatever help I needed.

As our relationship grew, those problems came out. Anxiety overtook me. I was constantly afraid of him even though he gave me no reason to be whatsoever. I would end up trying to bypass these fears by blaming him for things. Looking back on it, I was angry with him. Angry with him for not helping me achieve the perfect, healthy relationship that I deserved. Angry that things weren't easy. I was so tired of feeling so hurt all the time and so afraid. And I took this out on him, even though I didn't know it, and he didn't deserve it. Okay, a couple times, he wasn't so perfect. I still held it against him in a way that benefitted no one. Any mistake he made, I used as a shield to deflect from my real feelings.

And the anxiety was overtaking all parts of my life. My kids could see it, my coworkers could see it. I started to doubt that I would ever be able to have the healthy relationship I dreamed of.

It felt as though all the healing I had done had been for nothing, as if it was all just fake. And it was so frustrating. I could physically feel him resenting me, and that terrified me (even though he didn't resent me, I sure as heck thought he did). And truth be told, if things would have continued on as they were, he may have gotten to that point.

Through all of it, I blamed my ex, and I blamed my boyfriend – my ex for causing all this pain, and my boyfriend for not being able to help me fix it. But it was not his pain to fix.

My Heck Freaking No Moment came one afternoon. There was nothing particularly special except that the previous day, my friend from high school had done a Facebook Live about a life coaching program she was enrolling people in to heal their trauma and manifest their best life. And I thought, *Huh, that sounds interesting.* I wasn't fully sold on doing it. It was an investment, and I didn't know if I was ready to make that investment just yet.

Then my boyfriend and I got in a fight. I literally don't even remember what it was about, but I remember that I yelled at him. I mean, really yelled. Yelled like my ex used to yell at me.

I absolutely crumpled. It was like I heard myself from an entirely different planet. I made the choice then and there that

that was not the person I was going to be in my love life. I enrolled in the program the next day without hesitation.

I did that program and it changed everything. I stopped living in fear of my anxiety and started to *actually* heal on a deeper level. When that program ended, I wanted to know more. I enrolled in as many programs as I could afford. I became an energy healer and got involved in a healing circle in my town. I took more online coaching programs and classes in everything from tapping to YouTubing, and not only did I change dramatically, but so did my relationship. But there was something missing.

I was still not fully healing, and partly because so many of the programs that I was going through took the entire energy healing process so freaking seriously. And I just couldn't fully get into that.

I had spent so much of my life being serious that I had a really hard time getting into something under the pretense that it was "going to be painful," or "going to be hard to get through, but so worth it." I didn't like that one bit. That was also the reason that I wasn't a huge fan of therapy. Don't get me wrong, I think therapy is great! I have seen it help many people, but it wasn't something that I ever found worked for me.

Then one day I had a realization. I was listening to a podcast about Live Action Role-Playing (LARPing). They were saying that after a LARP, people sometimes have profound realizations about themselves. That is when it hit me.

You see, I have always been a nerd. I love fantasy worlds, and play Dungeons and Dragons with my kids regularly, and thoroughly enjoy a good video game or novel that takes me away to another world. But what I hadn't realized is that through all my classes and programs, I was using role-playing game strategy to help facilitate my own healing. And that if I needed my trauma healing to be fully impactful to me, I needed to make it fun. And I realized that I could make it a role-playing game. A *healing RPG!*

That was it. The start of my process. I worked diligently on nailing down all the most impactful tools that I had learned with, and also the ones that I had created myself or that were downloaded to me from the Universe (I am as much a lover of all things woo woo as I am all things nerd). And I compiled everything into a program, and then I added the fun. I created myself as a character in my own life, and magic happened. Not only did I heal in ways that I never could have thought possible, but I began manifesting things into existence at a rapid rate.

My relationship became so much more fun. It's healthy and happy and everything I ever dreamed it could be. It's truly the best I could have ever asked for.

All I needed was a story to make it possible. I needed to be my character. I used physical representations of my fears and battled them in my head. It was equal parts creative, artistic, and productive, all rolled into one amazing package.

I showed my process to people in my life who were suffering from trauma, and it helped them just as it did me. It has only grown from there.

That is why I wrote this book. I want to share this amazing fun with you. It is my mission to heal people through the power of play. I will stop at nothing to share this as far as I can!

I have seen the power of this program in action. It can not only heal your past, but also change your future and so, so much more than that.

Also, it's fun. And for me, that is the best part.

# How to Play the Game and
# Heal Your Pain

So, now that you see what I am all about (i.e., fun), I want to make sure that you are very clear on how this book, and game, works.

The first and most important thing to remember as you begin on the amazing anxiety healing journey that you are about to embark on is that this is a *game*! Don't forget that you are playing and having fun. The point of the whole darn thing is to be as creative as possible. It may sound odd, but I promise the deeper you go with your creativity, the more you will get out of the program. Let your inner nerd free!

Now, the next thing that you will need to do is get yourself a nice journal, something that makes you happy to write in. I always prefer leather bound myself, but yours could be covered in feathers and sing you a song when you open it. Whatever makes you stoked to open it is what we are going for here. And you can't have a good journal without an amazing pen! I am not going to lie, one of my favorite parts of life is finding those really good pens that make you never want to stop writing. No joke, I have *so many* pens because of this. So, get a pen (or many!) that makes you the happiest.

All right, now that I am confident that you have a suitable writing utensil, I can tell you about the fun part: how to play the game! Yup, here's your tutorial.

I want you to picture your favorite role-playing game, whether it be a video game or Dungeons and Dragons, or even the Sims, if that's your cup of tea. I want you to think about how that game works. It shouldn't be too hard; the premise of the game tends to be fairly simple as far as character development goes. They typically start you off with a base character, and maybe the only weapon you have is a stick and wooden shield or something of the like. Then, as you complete quests, your character earns experience points (XP) that helps them to gain levels. With each new level, they get new gear and skills. It's a pretty basic principle.

In *this* game, the entire adventure is centered on you being the character. Not only will you create a base-level character, but as you work your way through this process, you will learn new skills and the character you created will earn more gear. The only difference in this is that there are no experience points, you use each new skill you gain to signify to yourself that you have leveled up. There are ten levels.

On that note, you can't simply jump from Level 1 to Level 9 because you feel so inclined. You must do the steps in order. It is crucial for you to do this, not only because each level builds on each other, but because if you don't have the skills from the level before, there is no way that you will fully gain the skills needed to advance to the next one. Remember, it's a game – you can't take on the boss without leveling up first.

Not only that, but part of the process is to get very clear on where you are headed and what is holding you back. You must be very clear on both of these things in order to fully dive deep and heal the traumas that are causing your relationship anxiety. If you skip any part of this, you'll not only rob yourself of a fun experience but also the healthy relationship you desire.

As you work through the levels, there may be some skills that come easily to you while you might find others a bit more xxxii | Damsel No More!

challenging. That is perfectly and wonderfully okay and totally normal. It is not supposed to be the easiest thing you have ever done; if it were, you never would have gotten this book. Games that are too easy are no fun! However, if at any point you are feeling really challenged, be honest and kind with yourself. Don't get into the habit of judging yourself for anything that you feel come up during this process. Like any game, there are times when, though fun, something may make you want to throw your controller across the room and go eat ice cream. And that is fine, ice cream is amazing, but don't stop working through the process, for, as you will learn, those tough feelings are one of our greatest gifts.

This process is powerful. And without a doubt, if you lean in and follow the steps, the change in your relationship and your life will be profound. Through this process, you will finally get to feel what it is like to have a relationship where you don't fear your partner. One that is happy, where you feel comfortable and confident enough to communicate with your partner about your needs and wants.

That outcome may seem hard to imagine at the moment, but it is not a false promise. And the beauty of this game is that you can involve your partner in it, if you would like. You can share with them what you are doing *not* by talking about you directly, but about your character. The skills she has learned. The tools she has gathered. What she is achieving.

One more thing to note before we get started: each upcoming chapter is narrated with a story line, like cut scenes. Now the story is a fun and powerful one and has engaging characters and development, but it is in no way meant to be your story if you don't want it to be. If you feel it comes easily to you, definitely use it to narrate your own growth; however, if you are inspired by your own story, by all means, use that as the setting for your character. You don't have to fit your musings into my head at all. However, I strongly recommend you build some sort of story around your character to better help move your journey along.

By the end of this book, you will have the knowledge and tools necessary to truly take on your relationship fears. This feeling of truly taking back my life from my abuser is one of the most amazing things that I have ever experienced, and by the end of this book you will know how possible that is.

All right, ready, set, *go*!

# Create Your Character.
# Who Are You Right Now?

moke curls up into the dim gray morning light. It's both lucky and unlucky that it's raining. Lucky in the sense that the rain has stopped the fire from consuming your entire house, but unlucky that you are now staring at the carnage of your ruined home from the muddy dirt road, dripping as the sky releases its sorrow. If this had been the first time the beast had ravaged your *village, you may have released yours as well. However, it's not the first time you have felt the destruction of the beast, or the second, or the third. In fact, you have lost count of the amount of times you have stared at the smoldering shards of the safe haven you had created for yourself crumbling before your eyes. How many people have you lost to the beast? How much of your own life have you given to building and rebuilding because of its ferocity?*

*But this time is different; you are done. Done with watching the beast destroy what you love, done with being at its mercy, done with feeling powerless. This time, you have had enough, and you are going to do something about it. You cannot leave; this is your home, this is your life. These people, ankle deep in the mud of the street, are your people. No, you think, there is another way. You are going to figure out how to take on the beast.*

———————————

There are a few ways you can react to the scene you have just read:

Way one: feel powerless, feel the rain smacking you in the face, the mud caked around your ankles. You are eager to take on the beast, but how are you supposed to do that when it just destroyed your home?

Way two: you feel ready, eager, like the rain is driving you on, pushing you to find a way, despite the mud, to stop your world from being destroyed time and time again.

Way three: you feel a perfect confusing blend of both things.

I have a secret to share with you, *all* the ways of feeling are completely valid. I know that jumping into this new adventure of healing can be daunting, and I also know that you are extremely motivated to do so because your relationship hangs in the balance, your life hangs in the balance, and you know that it is time. Time for you to make a change. Time to take on the beast.

"What's the beast?" you ask. Well, for that you will have to be patient. Don't worry; it's only a few chapters away. Right now you need to get crystal clear on where you are now and *why* you want to embark on this journey. I am going to give you some very important and powerful tools to help with this.

First off, I want to make sure you understand the importance of comprehending where you are in this present moment. All too often, we tend to assess where we are and *who* we are in the present moment by either our past or our future, i.e., where we have been or where we are going. Our traumas or our dreams. And both things are fantastic but also aren't who you are as a person right now. They are part of you, sure, but not who you are. In order for this method to be successful in helping your relationship and self to grow and become as healthy as possible, you must have a very clear grasp on the "character" that you are right now.

The first tool that I want to give you to assist with this process is to clear yourself. Clearing yourself is something that is essential prior to doing any work on yourself. The reason it is important is because human beings inherently absorb the energies of others. We are biologically inclined to do this. It's part of the way we survived when we were hunter-gatherers. Sensing and absorbing energy is a survival technique at its core; it is what allows us to communicate silently with others and what enables empathy. However, oftentimes, energy that we pick up from others throughout the day can attach itself to us and burden how we genuinely feel. When we clear these energies from our system, it allows us to focus on ourselves and our own feelings. It stops us from viewing other people's garbage as our own.

This tool is one of the most powerful things that you can have in your arsenal, and it's also one of the simplest. I have *tons* of tools and weapons that I have learned over my years of healing, but this is the one tool that even now, I use every single day without fail. This tool alone has made a huge impact on the way I process what I am feeling.

Ok, here we go.

Anytime you are feeling anything that may be hard or uncomfortable, I mean anything from mild anxiety to full-blown panic attacks, or you are preparing to do some healing work, you are going to take a moment and close your eyes. Then, either in your head or out loud, you say, "Any feelings that are not mine need to leave my body now," and envision light rushing down through your head, all the way through your body and down into the earth.

*Boom.* That's it. That simple tool will clear out any feelings that don't belong to you. Just try it a few times and you will be astonished what feelings leave when you do.

The reason I wanted to teach you this trick very first is because when you do the first step in this process, you need to be acting and thinking about feelings that belong to you and you alone. You don't want your healing to be mucked up by the yuck of others.

Now that you have cleared yourself of any pesky emotions that you may have picked up from the day, we need to get you completely clear on how you currently view yourself and your relationship. Be warned: during this process, you will want more than anything to talk about what you want or where you want to be instead of thinking critically about where you currently are. Part of this is because it is actually hard to take stock of our talents and shortcomings and, nine times out of ten, when someone is recovering from an abusive relationship, they have an incredibly hard time thinking about themselves as a whole. Abusers thrive on the fact that they rob their victims of a sense of self, instead making them the only priority in their victims lives and causing the victim to think everything they are is not important. But, as I hope you know, that is garbage. It is, however, a "program" or belief that you may have to overcome, so acknowledging that that programming may pop up in this process is important.

We are going to talk about where you are now in three parts; what is hard, what is easy, and what made you want to take on the beast. So get out your journal and snazzy pen, and here we go.

In your journal, I want you to answer the below questions:

In this moment, what do I not like about myself?
What do I not like about my life?

This may feel odd to you to be starting off with the negatives, especially if you have ever worked in a corporate environment – it may be opposite of the way most of your self-helpish activities have started. But there is a reason for this. It is typically easier to talk first about the negatives or things that are hard for us. I put this section first to allow your mind and spirit to get all your yuck out on paper so you don't discredit your talents later.

For question one, I want you to list everything that pops into your head, from acne to being bad at math to the fact that you can't stop crying when you get angry and everything in between. Just pour it all out onto the page. Remember, this is about you as a person, not about your life.

For question two, I want you to think about your life. What would you change? List everything about your life that is not what you want to be in your life. This could be that you don't like that you don't have a ton of girlfriends or that you are having a hard time with finances or just straight up that you don't like that you have to pay taxes. Put everything on the page. Write everything out even when it may feel silly. Be honest with yourself; there is no judgment here. We *all* have things we don't like about ourselves and our lives. It is totally normal to have a long list.

The next step is to think about the things you are good at. And, though I called this the "easy stuff" a little bit ago, these questions can actually be harder than the stuff that you don't like about you. This is because this step means you have to acknowledge that there are good things about you, there are things that you rock at, things that make you amazing.

So, next in your notebook, I want you to answer the below questions:

What do I really like about myself?
What do I really like about my life?

I know what you're thinking: *These questions look vaguely similar to the previous ones about the stuff I suck at.* To that I say, "Yes, my friend!" They are very similar for a distinct purpose that we will get to shortly. First, I want you to take the time to really think about what you are amazing at.

For the first question, you need to be honest with yourself. List every single darn thing you like about yourself, from the color of your hair to your ability to tell it like it is. You need to put it down on the page. And don't cut yourself short. Brag like heck. *Everyone* has things on this list. Same with the following question. What do you like about your life? What is amazing? Is it your supercool dog (a big awesome part of my life, for example) or that you and your partner watch anime every Friday night? Call out all the things that make your life fantastic.

Ok, so now that you have taken the time to put down your opinions of you on paper, there is something very powerful that I want you to think about before we move on to the "what made you want to take on the beast" section, or the Heck Freaking No Moment section.

After you have answered the previous questions, I want you to take a moment to think about how you spoke to you in your head during both sections. Take a second to ponder the below questions:

How did I talk to myself about the things I don't like versus the things that I do?

What was different in how I criticized myself vs. when I built myself up?

Go back and read through both sections; you will be surprised at the voices that come through. Take note of your inner monologue. It is important to see the differences here because the way you spoke to yourself in your head in both sections is literally how you speak to yourself all day, every day. And as soon as you acknowledge that voice and its tones, you empower yourself with the ability to change it.

I want to take a moment to point out the difference between the words *unique* and *weird*. Everyone longs to be unique, to stand out in a good way, a way that makes you special. But very few people eagerly seek to be weird. To be weird conjures up the images of being outcast, alone, not like everyone else in a way that is not good. Here is the kick though, both words mean the same exact thing. It's just the power that we give them that changes our perspective on them. It is the same with how we talk to ourselves. When you are thinking about what you don't like, you think in terms of "weird" (not that what we don't like is weirdness, just the negative connotation). When you are thinking about your talents, you are thinking in the positive connotation of "unique."

Keep this in mind when reading over your responses, and note when it occurs. It will be very helpful for you to be mindful of when you're in your day-to-day life and your inner voice springs up. Sometimes when my voice comes out, I actually ask myself, "Unique or weird?" to give myself some framework on how I am categorizing my thoughts in the present moment.

Now that we have figured out how you view yourself and how you talk to yourself, I want you to think about what brought you here, what made you pick up this book, what made you want to tackle the challenge of taking on this beast?

I lovingly call this the Heck Freaking No Moment. I addressed this a bit before, but to be clear, this is the moment that made you decide that you had to do something, or you would lose your current relationship. Lose your chance to have successful, healthy love. It's the thing that made you afraid enough or determined enough to do something. Truth be told, this doesn't have to be huge; it just has to mean something to you. Think of my HFNM that I mentioned a few chapters ago: it was me yelling like the bad guy, like the one thing that I never *ever* wanted to be. . .*ever*. That triggered everything. One of my client's HFNM was in the grocery store when she asked if it was okay to buy her favorite snack. Whatever yours is, I guarantee you have one.

Prior to my HFNM, I had spent a lot of my life believing in the concept of Prince Charming as the amazing armor-clad, horse-riding, sword-wielding champion that would swoop in and show me what an amazing relationship was. And in my HFNM, I realized that here was my knight. My Prince Charming. And I was yelling for a reason I could not discern. That is the power of the HFNM.

That was what caused me to take my first real, hard look at how I viewed my life and what I wanted to change.

So the next step in this process is to write down, in as much detail as humanly possible, what your HFNM was.

What happened?

How did it make you feel?

Why is it important that that moment doesn't happen again?

Keep whatever you write in a safe spot. And if at any time during this journey you get discouraged, I want you to go back and read it. Remind yourself why you are here and how important it is to you that you get to live the way you want. That you have the relationship you want. And the happiness that you deserve. That your HFNM doesn't keep happening.

Here is the fun part and what makes the game that is this book so amazing. It is time to create yourself as a character! *Eeek!* This is the best.

What you need to do is either find a photograph or draw a picture of yourself, or even find a magazine clipping of someone you would like to imagine yourself as. You need to take this image and put it up somewhere that you can see it. If you don't have space to do this on a wall or mirror, do it in a binder or notebook, but keep in mind that you will need to leave yourself space to add things to this picture as you grow.

You are building a character. This is you at the beginning of the game. You have recognized you need to take action, you are going to conquer the beast, but currently you're muddy and drippy and don't have all the tools you need. But you are determined. Make this picture of you as plain as possible. Just you standing there. You will be adding to it. We are talking a no-skins-yet, Level 1 character. Because that is where you are starting in this game. You have officially entered the game as a Level 1 character, congrats! Now that you are here, we can start playing and getting you some of the gear you need. So put that picture up and start to really think about the character you want to become.

Add the magic of fun to it! Notice I didn't really give you many rules outside of leaving room for you to expand on your base-level character. Meaning, don't hold yourself back! Do you want your character of you to be an elf? Are you purple? Would you like to be the opposite gender? Perhaps you are a dwarf? Whatever you would like to be, you get to be. Throughout this journey, you will build on your character more and more as you build on yourself.

Remember, this is a game, which means that even when it's hard, remember you can make it through. And enjoy the adventure. You may be muddy now, watching the flames burn all you thought you had, but don't worry. You are embarking on a mission to get back all you have lost. Now, let's get to Level 2.

# Your Fear Monster and How It Is Affecting Your Relationship

*Y*ou scrounge what you can from the ashes of your home; it's not much, but it doesn't need to be. What little belongings you take, you strap to your back and set off toward the nearest town. Despite the weight on your mind, your limbs move easily, driven with intent. Before you can take on the *beast, you need to learn more about it. Where did this beast come from? Why is it here? Is there a way to kill it, to stop it from ever ravaging your village again? You know what your first stop will be: the tavern. Its darkened windows and desolate patrons make it the ideal place to begin when needing any information. All you need to do is drink and listen, sooner or later information will come from a traveler or merchant. Then you will decide what it will take, how you can prepare.*

*You thrust your soaking cloak onto a hook as you enter the tavern, sending droplets of water splattering onto the floor. There is a group of people already loudly arguing about the beast.* Perfect, *you think. You take a seat at the bar, order an ale, and begin to casually ask the tavern owner his thoughts on the rowdy conversation and the beast in general.*

———————————

All right, I know what you're thinking: *Can we learn what you mean by the beast yet?* The answer is, *yes*! Now, it's not as easy as me simply saying the beast is _____ and then sending you about your way to go vanquish it. This chapter, lovingly called the Fear Monster chapter, is where you really get to dive into – you guessed it – your fears! Yay!

Okay, I know now you are probably wondering why the heck I am stoked to talk about what scares you, but I really love this part. Here is why. Fear is an incredibly powerful thing. In fact, one of the most powerful emotions you can feel. There are two types of fear, *real* fear and *fake* fear, but without being aware of their differences, it is incredibly hard to identify which type of fear you are feeling at any given moment. Here is a quick way to tell the difference between the two. Get ready. When you are afraid, the easiest and quickest way to identify what fear you are experiencing is to ask yourself the lovely question, "What are my current chances of death?"

Yup, real fear means that your chances of death, or extreme maiming, are high. Like, real high. So high that you probably shouldn't need the question in the first place. However, fake fear can sometimes feel like real fear. In fact, when you first start out with this process, you will be shocked with how often you ask yourself this question because your brain didn't understand that your chance of death is not high.

Being an abuse survivor can make this incredibly difficult in a relationship situation. I often say that I had PTSD and I didn't know I had it until I was truly loved by someone. That is sad. True love brought out this crazy set of blinding and wild fears that I thought I didn't have due to the fact that when I was single, there was no reason for them to exist. The second that someone cared about me and didn't want to use me for their own game, my Fear Monsters had a heyday. Abusers have this terrible way of brainwashing us into believing that all fear is real fear because not pleasing them will "literally" equal death. In some cases, that is definitely true, but your abuser's biggest power play was to keep you in this constant state of fear. Because, as Anaïs Nin states, "Anxiety is love's greatest killer." Loving yourself or having any sort of confidence or freedom is a huge threat to those that want to keep you oppressed, such as, you guessed it, your piece-of-crap abusive ex.

Now, these fears that you got gifted by that gem are only *some* of your fears. You, like every other human on the planet, has scads of other fears. Seriously scads. Some of them you probably have never even truly identified as fears because you have become so accustomed to coddling them in your daily life. So the first step in identifying your beast or Fear Monster is to compile a big messy list of everything you are afraid of.

Notebook time! Get out your notebook and wonderful weapon of wording, aka your pen of choice, and open to a clean page. At the top of the page write "I am afraid of:" and then start to write down everything that pops into your head. Everything. The purpose of this is to vomit all your fears onto the paper. So if clowns comes out, that's great. Your great aunt's basement? Also fantastic. That you will push everyone in your life away? Perfect. Just put every fear down on the paper, and whatever you do, do not judge yourself. Don't. Like, not at all. About anything you put down.

If at first you don't know what to write, list the things that everyone is afraid of. Like being kidnapped or house fires or your mom dying. This gets your brain into the mode of thinking about the stuff that it hates to think about. But as you get into it, you want to not just think of the external things but also the fears that spring up in your relationship specifically. That will give you the biggest insight into the specific negative mental programs your ex gave you later on down the line.

Take as long as you need to make this list. Don't limit yourself. Let yourself express everything you feel that you need to. However, if you are having trouble getting your brain to give you your fears, it can help to set a timer. Fifteen minutes is a nice start. Tell yourself that you are committing to writing your fears for fifteen minutes, and then do it. If you write past the timer, that's great! The goal is just to get all your fears out there. This is also a running list, meaning if other things come up as you're walking your dog or eating your breakfast, throw them in! And don't forget to clear yourself before writing down your fears!

Then, once you feel you have at least a mostly complete log of all your fears, or a base level of fear vomit on the paper, read back through it. From top to bottom. Then you need to ask yourself which fears are based in real fear. Getting kidnapped, for example, or gun violence typically fall into this category. Go ahead and write those fears on a new page as a separate list or circle them. Do something that eliminates them from your immediate thoughts as you view your list.

The next step is to take your list and put each fear into categories based on how badly they scare you. I like to categorize my fears with a numbers system like one through five, but some of my clients have preferred to name their categories. One even used the baby shark song. If you don't know what that is, definitely Google it; it will be stuck in your head for hours.

If using the number system, a fear in category one would be something that has very little effect on you and your relationship or everyday life, such as clowns or an irrational fear of airport metal detectors (which I totally have never ever had by the way). A five on this scale is a fear that actually affects the way you act in your relationship or in your life on a day-to-day basis, like the fear of not being in control or the fear of angering your partner or the fear of an anxiety attack.

It is important to note that all fears are valid fears. All fears are valid fears. This does not mean that you *should* be afraid of what you are, but that when you *are* afraid of something, you truly are afraid. And that is not something that you should gloss over. Being afraid is visceral, and whenever you are afraid, you need to be sure that you are not beating yourself up for feeling that fear. I will give you further tools for this later on, but what I am saying right now is basically that your fears are real to you even when they aren't Real Fear in the sense that we have been speaking. And you have a right to your fears just as you do your happiness. Don't judge your experience of fear based on the experiences of others.

Now that you have your fears categorized, for the purpose of this adventure, you want to turn your attention to your category five or Grandpa Shark fears. Any of the fears on your list can be your beast, your ultimate Fear Monster. Any of them are that powerful in your everyday existence. However, I recommend picking one fear as your initial focus when going through this process for the first time. This game that we are playing is repeatable, and each time you use it, you will grow and be able to take on more and more fears. However, it is best to start with just one major fear. One fear that you feel is hurting you and your relationship the most. The one that makes your chest tighten the most.

Once you have decided which fear that is, you want to underline and bold it, write it on a new page. Whatever it is, you want to focus your mind on conquering that monster. I am not saying that, as other fears come up as we continue leveling up, you should push them aside and not take care of them, but merely that you know that your main foe is the fear you choose now, at least for the moment.

So, just like we did with you in the last chapter, you now get to create your Fear Monster on paper. You can't exactly find a photograph for this part of the game, but you can draw your monster or find a picture online that you can print out, or a crazy magazine clipping. Put it opposite your character of you on your wall or in your notebook. You can also put your monster on a separate page if you feel so inclined, but you want it to be very near where you placed your initial character.

You definitely want to create your Fear Monster exactly as it is: scary. I have seen people use dragons or ogres or random creatures that they create using parts of other creatures; whatever inspires you is just fine. This is a rather unique part of our game because in typical role-playing games, you get to create either the hero or the monster, but hardly ever both. But in this game, you have the power to decide what you are taking on. You will conquer this beast. Make it a mean one!

Once you have your beastly, monstrous image, you will want to name your beast. Write the name of your creature near it on the paper and write your actual fear near it as well. I like to have my character and monster on opposite sides of a paper personally, because then the entire time that you are gaining tools in this process, you can see your monster and what you are up against and so can your character. Have fun with the name of your beast, you will be the one to vanquish it after all, and you're going to want to add that monstrous monogram to your title.

Lean into this part of the process, be creative with all aspects of it. Give it your all to make your monster a foe worth defeating on paper with the same intensity that the fear is a fear worth defeating inherently.

The fact that you now have full knowledge of your fears will be incredibly helpful in your journey to overcome them; however, simply knowing your fears is not enough. Taking action is so important. One of my favorite quotes of all time addresses this more beautifully than I ever could. It states, "Fairy tales do not tell children the dragons exist. Children already know that dragons exist. Fairy tales tell children the dragons can be killed." G. K. Chesterton said this, and I love it so much that I even got part of it, the "dragons can be killed" part, tattooed on my arm. It eloquently demonstrates the need to take action when encountering a fear.

Now that you know your fears, you will actually be able to learn how to conquer and overcome them as you progress through this book. Knowing your Fear Monster is like the dragons in fairy tales; you now know they exist so that you may vanquish them.

———————————

*As the tavern owner pours you a second pint, he tells you all he knows of the beast. Many have tried to kill it, but no one has yet to succeed. He tells you of its secretive nature and massive stat-*

*ure. He says that he thinks the best chance anyone has would be if someone were brave enough to take it head-on. To go to its cave and stare it down.*

*"It likes to hide," he says.*

*You snicker.*

*"That may be so," you state, "but it isn't going to hide from me. I am going to drag it out. To force it to face me in head-to-head combat. I am going to battle the beast."*

*He raises his eyebrows in surprise but doesn't discourage you. Instead, he directs you to speak with the innkeeper on the other side of town. He says that last week she mentioned that some traveling knights had told her where to find the beast. But as you stand to leave, he grabs your arm, suddenly fearful of the beast himself. He tells you of its gnashing claws and fiery breath, its horns and wings and eyes that burn at your soul. You smile. You already knew those things, and you are prepared to train against them, to show the beast that you are powerful, too. You are not afraid, as the barkeep is. You are done with fear.*

---

This knowledge alone levels up your character. You have gained intel, a valuable asset in your journey. Now you can start to plan your approach, you can create a plan, the next step on your quest. You have achieved Level 2.

Level 3:

# Discover Your Quest by Setting Your Intentions

*he inn is quiet when you enter. The innkeeper sits behind the desk, reading something on a scroll of parchment. You have known her for a long time. She smiles when she sees you, the lines at the corners of her eyes creasing, but soon her smile turns to confusion as she sees your intent look of determination. She is a kind woman and immediately asks you what's wrong.*

*You tell her of your desire to take on the beast, and you ask if she knows anything about it or its whereabouts. The keeper thinks for a moment before closing her eyes and nodding.*

*"Wait here," she states.*

*She disappears up the stairs for a few moments before returning, a thick fold of paper in her hands. She hands you the parchment and you open it. It was left behind by some travelers long ago. It's a map to the wizard of the forest. The one that lives in the darkest part of woods, practicing ancient magic. He will help you become powerful enough to take on the beast.*

*You smile.*

———————————

Any good game has one amazing thing in common: an epic quest! This is a goal that you must achieve in order to win. It's the driving force of all the mini quests and objectives that you complete along the way. And just like any good game, you need to establish very clear and concise goals for yourself as you work through this program.

Before we get to how you will establish your goals or intentions, I want to tell you the story about the power of imagination. Awhile ago, I was very eager to understand and establish my "powers." Basically, I knew that I had some varieties of spiritual gifts, but I had been shoving them down for years, and now that I wanted to, for the life of me I couldn't dredge them back up. I was part of an awesome group filled with wonderful magical women, and I felt out of place, like I was failing or far behind. I saw a video about energy healing and immediately knew that I absolutely *had* to learn more about it. It was such a big pull, in fact, that the very next day, I signed up for a certification course. The main appeal to me about energy healing was that everyone could do it. You didn't have to have a specific set of gifts; it appealed to my feelings of not being powerful enough to help people. And energy healing is *amazing*. It's powerful and helped me create a deep and meaningful connection with Source or Creator.

I won't go into the details of what energy healing is here, but of all the lessons that I have learned through being a healer, one stands out as something all people on this planet should know: the power of imagination.

When I went for the certification course, the first thing we talked about was the power of imagination to create reality. To say that at first I had a ton of resistance to this concept is an understatement. Don't get me wrong, I have always loved imagination. Always. I was the kid who would read a fantasy novel, say, *The Chronicles of Narnia*, and spend months afterward looking in closets and reaching down squirrel holes hoping desperately that I could find a way to that amazing magical place. Even into adulthood, part of the reason that I still connect so intensely with imaginary worlds is because my heart loves magic. It loves the creativity that comes from the minds of others. I easily get enraptured in a good anime or book and lose myself in that world with ease.

But when studying healing, I learned that imagination was not just a tool used to create a fun experience. When done correctly and with dedicated intention, imagination can shape your reality.

If you really think about it, this concept isn't all that out there. In fact, it actually makes sense. Take, for example, when you need to have a difficult conversation; you spend a ton of time prior to when the conversation takes place imagining all the outcomes or ways that the conversation could go. So even when it doesn't go the way you expected, the fact that you used your imagination to prepare actually shaped the way that you dealt with the situation.

We are just taking that concept a bit further. I don't want you just to imagine outcomes and hope for a good one; I want you to have the power to create for yourself the things you imagine through strong intention setting, or manifestation.

In Level 1, you wrote down why you were here and what about your life you want to change. But now I want you to think about this, not what you wish would happen but what you are going *to make* happen.

Let me be very clear about one thing: there is no intention that is too large. You do not, under any circumstances, need to dream small. Don't limit your intentions for how you would like to live or what you would like to have in your life based on the belief that there is a limit to what you can attain. Often we hold on to the belief that there is a limit purely because other people in our life have instilled in us their fear of our success, making them feel challenged. Before you set and as you set your intention, it is important that you acknowledge if you hold that belief.

If you feel resistance to setting intentions, that's all right. As you set more and more, you will be able to work through that easily. However, it is important that you note those resistances as they pop up.

We are going to think of intention setting as a quest. Think of your favorite video game, anime, show, or novel that has a quest. If the quest was easy to achieve, the main character would simply pop to the final battle and, with a flick of their finger, defeat the final boss (*poof* – bye-bye, Voldemort), and the adventure would be over. First of all, how boring would that be? Like, really super boring. Second, that is simply unrealistic. The main character always, and I mean always, encounters difficulties along the way that they must navigate, but as long as they continue to move forward, they eventually make it to the final battle and have the strength to achieve what they initially set out to, even if it all doesn't happen the exact way they planned it to originally.

I want you to think about your intention setting, your quest, in a similar manner. When you set your intention for what you want and start on this journey, challenges are going to pop up. But as long as you keep moving in the direction of what you want, as long as you don't decide "Nah, I'll just go back home and let the beast burn my house whenever he would like," you *will* reach your final battle. You will achieve what you want to.

That is the power of your imagination. It can genuinely shape your reality into what you dream it to be.

The first step in setting a powerful intention is to come up with a validation. A validation is something that you ask the Universe to send you to let you know that you are on the right path. Something that sends you the sign that, even when you feel discouraged, you are doing what you are supposed to. The magical part of selecting a validation is that, the second that you establish what your validation is, you will see it pop up *everywhere*. It's sincerely amazing.

Your validation could be everything from butterflies to the number 7. My personal validation is rainbows. When I first decided on rainbows, I was concerned. My thought was basically, *How am I going to see rainbows if it barely ever rains here?* But I really felt that that was what my validation needed to be, so

I went with it. And that evening, when my kids came home from school, my oldest daughter excitedly pulled her drawing that she had made at school out to show me. It was literally twenty rainbows covering a page. I cried.

That is the power of setting a validation. In order to set a validation, simply decide what your personal validation will be and write in your journal, or on a napkin, or on your hand, basically anywhere, "When I am on the right path, Universe (or Creator, Source, God, or whatever you resonate with), please send me _____." And that's it. You will see it pop up everywhere.

Next, you need to decide what your intention is going to be. You can basically choose whatever you would like for your intention. It can be one thing, like no longer having anxiety, or many things, like getting a new job, having a healthy relationship, and making 10,000 dollars a month. Whatever matters to you is what you should set for your intention.

Now in order to establish your intentions – the end goal of your quest – you are going to sit down and write yourself a letter.

This letter is to you as you are in this moment telling yourself what you are going to achieve by working through this program. Start your letter however you would like. Dear Me, Dear Self, and Howdy Partner are all viable options. Then you are going to write about what you are feeling now and why you want to change those feelings. Write about why it is important to achieve what you want, and then, and this is the important part, write what you want. Write it not in the way that you imagine scenarios, i.e., without words like *hopefully*, *maybe*, or *I wish*. You must write down your intentions as things that are *going* to happen. Even if they sound crazy. Write them down because you want them. And because you want them, know that they are *going* to happen. You will reach your intentions. Period.

Writing them down affirmatively helps not only your brain but also the Universe understand that these are things that are a reality, not a wish.

Next you are going to take your letter and put it in an envelope. Seal it up. Or fold it into a paper crane if you don't have an envelope on hand. Just make it a sealed paper. This is not so that you forget your intentions, as obviously that is not the goal. The reason that you need to seal up the letter is because it is going to create a concrete goal, a physical, real thing that you get to do when you feel you have completed your quest that your brain immediately recognizes as a tangible reward.

You will keep your sealed letter with you in a place where you won't lose it. Wherever you would like to keep it, make sure that it is safe. Then, once you have worked through the processes in this book, you will get to open the letter. When you open the letter, it is going to be an incredible experience, rewarding in ways that you can't even fathom now. So even if you have the urge, do not open the letter until you know that you have reached your intentions, or you have a strong sign sent to you that it is time to do so.

One thing I want to make sure that you distinguish between during this process is the difference between intentions and expectations. Now as much as we all wish it did, the Universe never, ever, *ever* acts in the way that we expect it to. Which means that if you hold on to any expectations of how your intentions should be delivered to you, you are going to be brutally disappointed. Over and over again. It is not your job to decide *how* things are going to happen for you. It is instead up to you to let the Universe know what you have decided needs to happen, and then let the Universe provide it to you in the ways that it deems fit. Nothing will ever happen the way you want it to specifically. So let go of your expectations for how things must to come to you.

I am not saying that expectations for yourself and others are inherently bad; however, they often lead to disappointment. It is important that you take stock of your expectations and understand that often they are not reality. They can sometimes even come from programs that you have adopted that come from fear and are therefore not something you actually want to happen in your life.

So, as you write your letter, be sure you are not saying *how* your future is going to come, but more *what* will come. Establishing this knowledge will drastically ease your transformation in becoming the person that has what you want as opposed to being resistant to change.

Now once you have written your letter, you have officially started on your quest to your future. Congratulations, your character has leveled up once more. It's time to go get some gear!

―――――――――――――

*As you leave the town, you see the forest looming in the distance. It's dark and the trees twist out in different directions, creating spires that strike fear into most. But you aren't afraid; you are optimistic. You can feel the winds of change, of power blowing through your hair, ruffling your edges. You hear the sounds of birds chirping and leaves rustling. The reign of terror of the beast is ending. You can feel it. You look at the map. It will be the first time that you have met a wizard. You wonder what knowledge he will give you but know without a hinderance of a doubt that whatever you learn will take you ever closer to your goal. Your destiny is happening now, and you cannot wait.*

# How to Make the Hidden Magic of Anxiety Work for You

You have never been this deep into the forest before, you think to yourself as you press on following the map. The trees twist together and the brush clings to the earth in large masses, making the hike toward your destination treacherous. You know you are getting close. You just have to be. There are noises *here. Noises that you haven't heard before. Yips and creaks and rustlings. You keep your mind focused, trying to push the fear you feel from it. Clutching the map, taking the forest one step at a time.*

---

Now that you know where you are going, we get to start on this fantastic journey to your healthy, anxiety-free relationship. In order for you to move through your anxiety and fear, and frankly every emotion that may ever come up, you will need to have a better understanding of what emotions are.

Emotions are one of the greatest gifts that we are given as human beings. They allow us to connect with one another in profound ways; they enable art to exist; they are even our GPS system directing us forward toward creating the life we want. They are powerful frequencies that direct us to see what needs to be healed within our lives and show us our next steps.

Let me break it down like this: Emotions are like the radio. Let's say you are driving along, listening to your local country music radio station. You are really liking the songs that they are playing at the moment. You're jamming out, giving your steering wheel quite the concert. Now, just because you are currently listening to the country station, does that mean that the pop station or the rock station or NPR are completely gone? Just, *poof*, shut off because *you* aren't listening to them at the moment? No, they are still existing. They are just on different frequencies.

So, if all of a sudden a song comes on the country station that you just can't stand, what would you do? You would change the channel. That is how your emotions work.

Your emotions are frequencies just like different radio stations. Even if you aren't feeling something at the present moment, it doesn't mean that that emotion it is gone; you just simply aren't tuning into that frequency at the given moment. And the beauty of this is that you are the master of your dial. You have the power to change your frequencies when you would like, and once you acknowledge this power, that is when you start to fully grasp your God-given magic.

Now I am not saying that when you feel anxiety or fear or sadness you should just *boop* ignore that and hop on over to the pop station. No, not one bit. In fact, I am actually saying quite the opposite. In order to change the channel, it's not as simple as just saying you don't want to feel something anymore and burying it away. That will cause all sorts of issues. When we shove down our emotions or "bypass" them, we aren't actually switching the channel, we are just trying to play a different station in our headphones as the car radio plays. No matter how noise-canceling the headphones are, you are never fully able to drown out the sound. This is also where problems like overeating come from, because we are so full of emotional chaos and turmoil that we haven't dealt with, we turn to things that help us drown out the station we don't want to hear, such as the comfort of a candy bar. Bypassing an emotion never works in solving any problem. Sure, there may be times in your life when you need to bypass for a moment, but it is important that you are aware of these times so that you can return to the emotion later when you have a moment to properly sort through what it is telling you.

Yup, emotions tell you things all the time. This may sound like a simple concept, but oftentimes it is hard to discern what in fact your emotions are saying or showing you. The first step in what you are being shown is to get a full grasp on how you are feeling. And I am going to let you in on a major secret that you may not like so much. The emotions that are the hardest to feel are the ones that are the most valuable. Your emotions are your magic, and your deepest, darkest, most intense emotions are your most powerful spells. The secret in changing everything about your life lies in those emotions. Some people call the more dense emotions your "shadow." If that term resonates with you, by all means, go for it! But for me, that term never made a ton of sense. After all, no developed character is all light or all dark, any compelling character is a blend of both, with aspects of the whole spectrum flowing through their entire being.

Think about some of these interesting blended characters. Did they have their most profound growth when they were experiencing times of light? The answer is usually no; it was when they were working through the denser, more difficult feelings that they truly achieved their potential. I know that it is much easier for us to see this when we are not in the heat of our own emotions. But here is a concept that I want to make sure you understand: dense does not equal bad. Dense simply equals, well, dense. The dark emotions are not bad emotions. It should never – under any circumstance – be your mission to eliminate them from your life, no matter how uncomfortable they may make you. No, the mission here is to understand what they are telling you so you don't get stuck in their density for uncontrollable amounts of time, so you can see and learn what you need to from them and then move on. All emotions are good emotions. Some are easier to feel than others because they are a lighter frequency; they are basically just easier for our minds, bodies, and spirits to digest. The denser ones are thicker like toffee and take longer to chew on and digest, which makes them uncomfortable for us to experience.

Sometimes it's easy for us to identify what we are feeling. If you're like me, when you were little, you were taught the basic five emotions: joy, disgust, anger, fear, and sadness, to which I also add love, as I believe it definitely is deserving. And that anything that you felt was an iteration of one of those types of emotions. I would beg to say that that is not necessarily true, and that all the frequencies of emotions do not stem from an overarching hierarchy of emotions, but instead are each their own unique type of magic spell. However, I am going to use the above six as examples in discussing this first exercise, because they are the ones that are the most identifiable for the largest number of people. Essentially, they are the "cleanest" to feel.

For this first emotional-magic exercise, you are going to connect your emotional frequencies with how they show up in your body. When we experience an emotion, our mind is not the only thing to react. Our bodies similarly demonstrate the signs of the frequencies that we are experiencing. Sometimes this is a fairly universal reaction, like increased heart rate when feeling afraid or smiling when happy. However, oftentimes our bodies will present us with unique-to-us signals of our emotions that we tend to gloss over with all the noise our minds are making about it. It is important to connect to your body so that you can be fully present when navigating the magic of your emotions.

I want you to find a quiet space where you can have your journal nearby, and that you are comfortable in. The first thing that you need to do is decide which emotion frequency you would like to experience. Then, once that is selected, I want you to close your eyes and clear your energy (as we learned in Level 1), and then take five deep, long breaths. In for eight, hold for eight, out for eight. Once you have taken your breaths, and you feel aligned, I want you to think of the strongest memory you have for when you felt your selected emotion. For example, if you have decided you would like to experience joy, first you will think of the absolute happiest and most joyful memory you can. I want you to sit there in that memory. Try to remember all you can about it that made you feel your specified emotion. Wrap yourself in it, let it surround you. Once you feel completely enveloped, I want you to turn your attention to your body. What about *your body* specifically is feeling this emotion? How is your breathing, your heart rate? Do you feel your fists clenching or a knot in your stomach? What temperature are you? Do you feel pressure in any one part of your body? What does your throat feel like? If you are familiar with your Chakras, how are they reacting? Take stock of everything you feel in that moment. Then, when you feel that you have a good grasp on what your body is feeling, I want you to repeat the initial breathing exercise that you started with to reground yourself to the present moment.

Before you move to the next emotion, you want to list everything you felt in your body when feeling your specified emotion. Each time you do this for a different emotion, you are essentially creating emotional cheat sheets for yourself. The more aware you are of how emotions physically show up for you, the easier it will be for you to identify the way that you are feeling when in the heat of a moment.

I suggest doing this exercise first with the six emotions that I mentioned above, just to get yourself acquainted with the process of this exercise. However, you by no means have to limit yourself to just those emotions. At any time, you can expand to other emotions and do this exercise, and you will continue to help yourself better understand how you react to frequencies.

You can also do this exercise right after you have experienced a powerful emotional spell, like after an argument with your partner or a bad day of work. You can note what your body is currently feeling to help you better connect with your way of processing.

Doing the feeling work in the body will also help you hear your emotional frequencies more clearly, because you are not just focused on what you are thinking, but instead experience your emotions with your whole being.

As you continue through this game, we will dive deeper into what your emotions are showing you, but for the moment, I want to talk about true emotions vs. valid emotions. I know that sometimes, especially when dealing with anxiety, it is easy to start thinking that you are acting crazy, that you shouldn't be feeling the way that you are. We all have that voice in our head from time to time, but even when our logical mind says, "Why are you feeling this, you shouldn't be," we still feel everything that we are. This is because every emotion, *every emotion*, that we feel is a *valid* emotion. We have a reason for feeling it, even if it is not what we are currently thinking it is, and that is why we continue to feel it. Every emotion has a purpose and is valid when it arises.

This does not mean that every emotion we feel at all times is *truth*. Here is the difference: Let's say that you feel angry because someone hit your car while you were shopping and didn't even leave a note. Yes, that anger is a valid, real feeling and serves a purpose, but it may not be leading you to the truth. In your anger, you think that you just have bad luck, or that no one respects anyone anymore. Those things aren't truth. And just because you are currently feeling angry, someone else, or even you on a different day, could come out of the store to have their car hit and react in a completely different fashion.

We are going to talk about what triggers your emotional responses in the next chapter, but one quick and easy way for you to prevent your emotions from overrunning you is what I call minute meditations. As I have stated, it is very important to make sure that you allow time for yourself to feel what you need to, but there are some times when you need to put an emotion away to experience at a later time. One easy way of doing this is to clear your mind by thinking of nothing but your breath. To do this, just take a moment and go to the bathroom, or the broom closet, or it can be as simple as just closing your eyes.

Then just breathe, and inside your mind, say, *breathe in, breathe out*, and do so. Think of nothing at all but saying those things to yourself. Don't let a breath go undescribed. Do this for anywhere from one to five minutes. This will help you to get a better grasp on what is happening in the moment and give you time that you need to continue about your day. This is a conscious decision that you are making to let yourself feel what you need to, but just not at the moment.

--------

*The denseness of the forest grabs at your senses. The farther you fight your way into the thick mass of life, the more apprehensive you get. You must make it to the wizard's house; you must slay the beast. You push on deeper, following your map, hypervigilant of the terrain around you. You feel it first, as if a wall of invisible energy washes through you. Then you see it, a clearing with light, beautiful warm light, pouring in through the branches above. You left the town hours ago. You feel it, this is your destination. Unconsciously, your hands release their grip on the parchment. You don't notice, you are transfixed on the scene before you.*

*In the middle of the clearing, there is a small house with smoke eagerly fluttering from the chimney. An old man is standing in the doorway. He looks at you expectantly, as if he has been waiting for you, wondering what has taken you so long. And also, as though he has known you for many years. As you step into the clearing, a sensation moves through your body. You look down at your hands; they are glowing. In finding this place, you have crossed the first threshold. You have discovered your magic, and the wizard knows it.*

---

Now that you have your magic, it is important that you give the character of you her magic as well! Have fun with this (yup, more fun, the whole book is about it)! Don't take magic, of all things, too seriously. On your character image, draw, cut out from magazines, or print pictures of the magic you would like to have. Remember this is your character, you want to have fire power? Sweet, draw some flames! You would prefer to wield a Harry Potter–esque wand? *Do it!* Shapeshifting? *Boom*, you are a wolf! There are no rules on the type of you that you can be; just be sure that you take the time to level up your character to Level 4 with some wicked powers for the warrior you are!

Level 5:

# Find Where Your Triggers Are Hiding

S weat drips down your brow as you stare at the wizard. He is taking great pleasure in being your teacher, but learning to master your powers from him is not proving to be easy work. You have been here a week now and still feel little difference from the moment you walked into the clearing. The wizard's ideas of teaching are not what you had in mind. He bade you put *a new roof on his cottage using only one arm, not helping as he transformed into a bird and flitted about your head squawking loudly. One evening, he spilled a large pot of grain on the floor and instructed you to pick it up grain by grain, only for him to spill it again once you had neared completion. When he decided it was time for actual training, he would leave you largely weaponless or give you small items like a handheld knife or sharpened branch and demand you cause him to fall, as he did nothing but dodge your blows and blasts of magic by effortlessly displaying his own. You stare at him. While he plays his stupid games, the beast ravages your village, your people growing hungry time and again. This time, you must make him fall. Today's "weapon" is a club made of wood that is rough against your callousing hands. You swing it at him, but in an instant, he disappears, reappearing behind you and swatting the back of your head. "Again," he states with a smirk. You grit your teeth.*

---

Now that you have learned how to identify and better understand your emotions when they arrive, it is time that we talk about triggers and boundaries.

Triggers are the specific things that happen in your life that cause an emotional reaction. Don't get me wrong, there are many, *many* different things throughout your life that can trigger you into differing states of emotional response. But for the most part, all triggers that send you into a dense frequency fall into one of these categories:

- Wound Trigger
- Boundary Trigger
- Identity Trigger

It is important to know each of the types of triggers so that when you are being triggered, you can better understand what that trigger and emotion are showing you. Before I speak about them, I want to make sure that you understand that triggers are not negative. Just like the concept of dense emotions, triggers themselves are not a bad thing. They are actually something that the Universe sends you to allow for an emotional response to show or lead you to what you need to know to progress forward. So, while triggers can often feel very painful and dense, they are truly something to be very, very thankful for. And you can be triggered into a less dense emotion as well – they don't happen exclusively for dense emotions. You can just as easily be triggered into love as you can into frustration. However, for our purposes, know that, unless I otherwise state so, when I am discussing triggers, I am talking about triggers that send you toward density.

The first type of trigger that you should be aware of are Wound Triggers. Wound Triggers occur when we are pushed into an emotional reaction that is showing us a wound from our past that needs to be healed. Let me give you an example of this.

When I first left my ex, I had varying Wound Triggers come up. These presented themselves through things like hearing songs that I had listened to with him or fearing going to places where he may be because his face was terrifying. These are common triggers for most survivors of abuse. And I actively worked through them. They were easy to identify – when I would get an emotional reaction from these things, I knew that the wound that they were showing me was abuse connected. As I worked more with them, I found these wounds stemmed from the pain I had experienced at the betrayal of loving someone who didn't love me back – not necessarily just because he was abusive. I discovered this because when one of these triggers occurred, I was aware of it and that it was leading me toward a wound. And once I was able to address that wound (don't worry, the *how* of how I did that is coming up), I was able to move past those triggers being an issue. In fact, things like hearing his music or even seeing his picture don't trigger me at all anymore. However, I worked through much of those triggers during my single period, or The Great Reclaiming, as I genially have dubbed it.

The next triggers I identified were harder because they were the things that were popping up once I began a new relationship. I noticed (as I am sure you will notice now that you are aware) that the triggers that happen, specifically anxiety triggers, were from much deeper pain. I was getting severely triggered by things like not feeling heard or having everyone need something from me. Basically, the second that I couldn't fulfill what I deemed was important, I emotionally exploded. After a deep journey into myself, I was able to discover the wounds that needed to be healed that were coming up with these triggers, and they all essentially stemmed from my utter fear of not being valuable enough to be what everyone else needed.

These are what wounds look like. They are not so much a physical thing that was done to us, but rather our own thought process and internalization of that thing that caused us severe suffering. It is of value to note that some of these wounds may not be from what we deem the more "traumatic" experiences of our lives, but rather something that was caused within us based off countless small experiences. This is often the case with wounds that stem from the "not being enough" myth.

We can also be Wound Triggered in small ways. For example, whenever I am really into a show or anime (usually an anime), if they ever get into an arc or something that makes me uncomfortable, I mean the "Oh, no, that's not actually happening, they can't do that" feels we all get from the best-written shows, I used to just stop watching it for a while. I mean, with some of my favorite shows, I have stopped watching for extended periods of time because I was avoiding the feelings they were dealing with or presenting in the show. This was me being triggered. The fact that someone else was experiencing a feeling and I was witnessing it and it made me want to completely shut it out was clearly indicating that I had a wound around that particular feeling. It took me a bit of time to fully understand that was happening and is still something that I am actively aware of.

The second type of trigger is a Boundary Trigger. Boundary Triggers can sometimes be a bit trickier to identify than a Wound Trigger simply because they can sometimes lie below a wound. A boundary is something that you set for yourself about how you would like to be treated. This can be a guideline that you establish for others to treat you or for you to treat yourself. It goes without saying that boundaries are important – and not just important, but essential. I will go over in more depth in the next chapter about how to set and enforce boundaries, but you need to be aware that when your boundaries, your rules for how you want to be treated, get crossed, this will trigger you. And it should. This is what helps you to enforce your boundaries in the first place.

I discovered one of my major Boundary Triggers hidden beneath the Wound Trigger I mentioned above. The feeling of everyone needing something from me not only triggered my wound of not being enough, but once I had worked through that, I noticed it was also triggering my "I need help to get everything done" boundary, where I was feeling overworked and underappreciated. This led me to be able to communicate my needs in a way that was actionable and establish guidelines around getting those needs met.

The final type of trigger is an Identity Trigger. I like to think of this one as the hard-to-hear-icky-feedback trigger. This trigger occurs when something happens that challenges our sense of self. That bothers us because it is in direct conflict with what we view as our personal values. These triggers cannot be healed or boundaried away. They require action, and usually we are well aware of these triggers when they pop up.

My example of this comes from my time working in Human Resources. Part of the reason that I left the HR field is the "protect the company" concept that makes up the duality of the job. I was often triggered when I would want to do something or give an employee help that they needed for one reason or another that was in contrast with the company's bottom line. Whenever the bottom line came into play it bothered me, like a lot. One of my values as a person is compassion, and I simply couldn't stand the fact that the company was not doing what was best for the employee. Now, before I identified this as an Identity Trigger, I first made sure that this was not a Wound Trigger by ensuring that it was not coming from a place of ego. Though, truth be told, when you get triggered by an Identity Trigger, you will know. It feels different than a Wound Trigger because you are backed by the passion to act. In my case, furiously fighting for the employees and eventually a career change in order to help more people and not align with a machine.

When you are triggered in any of the ways above, it can be easy to want to turn to ways of not being triggered, like eating or social media. But that just keeps us in the cycle of not healing, and the Universe knows this and will continue to send us more and more triggering moments until we address what it is trying to show us. That is part of the reason for your Heck Freaking No Moment – the Universe knew that by sending you enough painful, difficult, triggering experiences, you would do something about it.

———————————

*You spin on your heels to face the wizard, yet this time pause a moment before attacking. He is smart, true, but so are you. Sure, you have never had combat training, but you can figure this out. You jump backward, away from him, hoping to gather your wits to create a better plan. He raises an inquisitive eyebrow. You circle him slowly. Pushing to see an opening, a way for you to get him. You feel your heart beat in your chest. In a rush, you lunge at him again, but your aim is slightly off. He vanishes in a flash of light. Perfect, you think to yourself. In a swift motion, you drop your club, letting the weight of it spin you around just as the wizard reappears in the space that was behind you. You throw your arms upward, blocking the smack he had intended to give and taking him by surprise. You knock him off kilter and cause him to lose his balance. With a rush of magical wind, he stops himself from fully hitting the ground, but rather floats a foot from it as if caught by a cloud. But you cannot see this, as before your eyes on your up-stretched arms shines the metal of a beautiful bronze shield glinting in the light of the clearing.*

---

Your character has leveled up once more! Throw a shield her way! There is a reason that I gave you a shield before any other piece of tactical equipment. A shield gives its wielder time to think and reason and plan. With your acknowledgment of what triggers you and why, you will have that ability. It is essential in battle and in your progression. Be creative! Be colorful and have fun creating your character's shield.

Level 6:

# How to Put on a Heavy Set of Boundaries and Communicate Them to Your Partner

*ou wake abruptly to the wizard shaking you. The world around you is still built of blurry shapes as you rub the sleep from your eyes and inquire about the abrasive awak-*

*ening. He smiles his wily, knowing smile that you have come to learn foretells a lesson with double meanings. Calmly, he details out his plan for the varying menial tasks that he wants you to complete that day and the necessity that you begin them at once. His list is long. Longer than any he has presented you with thus far. You are annoyed at hearing the list, not that any of the items are difficult to accomplish, more that they are meaningless, trivial tasks that don't seem to serve any real purpose. This is not why you came here. But he has agreed to teach you; there must be some point to all this absurdity.*

*As you begin working your way through the list, he continues to hover over you in his typical fashion, talking continuously about the same things that he has already told you more than once during your short time here. It has been about a week since you got your shield, and since that moment, the combat training has all but completely stopped. You are tired of this. How long does he expect this to go on? How long does he want you to stay and do his chores with your growth stalling by the moment? You have a mission to do. You are gathering up his laundry when he finally crosses the line. He "accidentally" bumps into you and scatters the damp laundry over the dirt.*

*"Unfortunate," he chortles. "Now you must do it all again."*

*You snap. In a whirlwind, you spin, throwing the basket toward him. Retorting on how it is not your job to relieve him of his daily tasks. Instead of asking him when he will actually show you how to use your magic, or more combat techniques, or, sky forbid, how to slay the beast, you simply straighten yourself up, look him dead in the eye, and say, "If you cannot help me defeat the beast as you stated you would, then I will take my leave to find someone who can. I am under no obligation to remain in your tutelage."*

*There's that smile again. Without words, he nods for you to follow him as he casually strolls toward the woods.*

---

As we dive into navigating your triggers, you probably have noticed that we are actually going to go a bit out of order. There is a rhyme and reason to this. The rhyme is that it is simply easier to work through Boundary Triggers first. The reason is because it is important for you to begin noticing your intrinsic boundaries.

1. Acknowledgement of them is essential to having a healthy relationship.
2. It will also help you see where your Fear Monster is lurking in unexpected places that can help you uncover more Wound Triggers.
3. Boundary Triggers help you start to explore the art of communication in a digestible way.

The first thing that we need to do when identifying and establishing boundaries is talk about all the areas in your life or times in your life that you felt overwhelmed or exhausted. When I first started this process, I felt overwhelmed and exhausted all the freaking time. I promise even if it feels daunting now, you will soon feel relief from this as you dive deeper into this boundary-building process.

In your journal, I want you to start a fresh page, and at the top write "Overwhelmed." Then I want you to write down any time that you recall feeling overwhelmed. You don't have to put a ton of detail into this, just list key times that you remember feeling this. I don't want you to write down the actual time that they occurred, like last Thursday at two p.m.; I am referring to recording specific situations in which you felt overwhelmed. So, if last Thursday at Beth's house you felt overwhelmed, write that down, but try and make sure whatever you write down will trigger a specific memory if you go back to read it next month. You do not need to have a comprehensive list of every time ever that you have felt overwhelmed or exhausted written on this paper. This is just a list of the immediate times that come to mind. Notice that *overwhelm* often feels like anxiety as well, so if you have times when you were overwhelmed with anxiety, write those down too.

The next thing that you need to do after you have recorded the times that you remember feeling overwhelmed is select one time on this list. Just one. It doesn't have to be the biggest or most painful example, but one that stands out clearly to you so that you can easily recall the situation. Then what you are going to do is write down what the situation was in detail. Don't judge anything you put down on the paper. Simply write down:

- How the overwhelm/anxiety started,
- What happened as it was occurring,
- How the overwhelm/anxiety ended,
- What you were thinking and reacting to during this experience,
- What you think about it now.

This may feel like a lot of questions to respond to at first glance, but when you get to writing, you will find that they all will naturally be answered the more you think about the situation, so don't stress on them too hard. Remember, these are your feelings. They are all valid. There is no right answer.

Once you have your situation clearly written out, take five grounding breaths (the eight seconds in, eight seconds hold, eight seconds out breaths). You are now going to read through what you have written down. I want you to look for the specific moment when you began feeling overwhelmed and why you felt that. Don't make it harder than it needs to be, this is usually very clear, but even after you have found it, read the entire situation through to the end.

Here is why: When you are in the moment, it is hard to discern which boundary is being crossed because your emotions essentially feel blinding. They are trying so hard to point out the problem that it is easy to get caught up in them and unfortunately miss the problem altogether. But we need our emotions to show us our boundaries, or else our boundaries wouldn't exist. Without the emotional tie to how we feel we need to be treated and cared for, it is nearly impossible to be passionate about it. Feeling overwhelmed is actually a very good thing, as it is an incredibly good indicator of a Boundary Trigger.

Next, after you identify when you got triggered precisely, I want you to write down how the situation could have gone ideally, in a way that would not have made you feel overwhelmed. Take your time to play out your options in your head; however, don't talk yourself out of ways that you would have preferred it to happen. We are looking for you to be authentic with you here.

After both situations – what happened and what you wished would have happened – have been written down, go back through and circle things that stand out to you. It may be very clear at this point what boundary was crossed, but sometimes it's not, and because our minds easily process stories, it helps us to clarify the main issue when we read through the outline and outcome concretely on paper.

Now it's time to try and put the boundary that was crossed into a *When/Feel* statement followed by an *It Is Important to Me* statement. This will help you to not only remember the boundary but also to see where the boundary comes from; i.e., is it trauma-based and therefore something that you need to work on with some of the tools I will give you in the next chapters, or is it something you need as a person? And once it is a clear sentence, it is drastically easier to communicate to your partner. Let me give you some examples.

Your boundary statement should look something like this:

<u>*When*</u> *people talk over me, I* <u>*feel*</u> *unheard.*
<u>*It is important to me*</u> *to feel heard.*

<u>*When*</u> *I don't see my partner helping with housework, it makes me* <u>*feel*</u> *like he doesn't care.*
<u>*It is important to me*</u> *to feel appreciated.*

<u>*When*</u> *my partner misunderstands me, I* <u>*feel*</u> *unimportant.*
<u>*It is important to me*</u> *to feel valued.*

Notice that in the above statements I could have said any number of feelings at the end of the *It Is Important to Me* statements that would be valid based on the *When/Feel* statements.

This is how it should be. You should be answering this for yourself. What you need and what you feel should be the focus. Also, notice that I didn't put the word *overwhelm* anywhere in the statements. This is because we tend to use *overwhelm* as a catchall word for *all* the feelings that are bombarding us (sometimes we use *anxiety* in a similar crutchlike fashion). It is important that you put into words the other emotions you feel when your boundaries are crossed, because *overwhelm* is not an emotion that people are able to understand in a way that will help you, and it is highly un-communicable what you mean when you say "I am overwhelmed." It can mean something different to every person you speak to. That is the reason you circle words and phrases that stand out to you in the situations so that you can start to mentally pull out what you are truly feeling from the bucket that is *overwhelm*.

This writing work may seem a bit lengthy, I am fully aware of that. But you by no means will have to do this forever. This is just a clear way to get to the *When/Feel* and *It Is Important to Me* statements, which we will now be calling a Boundary Statement, which is a little easier to type out. If you feel overwhelmed and anxious about something, and you can easily put what you're feeling into a Boundary Statement, by all means, do so. Do it now! But be sure that you still write down what that statement is, because you must have a clear grasp on it in order to communicate what you actually need from others and yourself.

So now here is the nitty gritty part of boundaries. In order for your boundaries to be respected, you must communicate what they are to your partner or to the other people, often relatives, that are crossing them in your life, and this includes yourself. If you don't both communicate your boundaries and needs and enforce the fact that they must be respected, no one will ever do so.

When communicating your boundaries, it is essential that you have a boundary statement to fall back on. The number one reason for this is because, oftentimes, informing someone of your boundaries is a triggering experience, especially after enduring an abusive relationship where literally nothing of anything that you needed or are was respected at all. It can be a *very* challenging feat to ask for the respect of your partner on something that bothers you and may be hard for him to understand. But you need to remember that you are worthy of having needs. Not just of having them be respected, but of having them period. It was easy to push your needs aside when you were forced to do so in order to gain the love of your partner in your previous relationship, but that is the number one reason you are having issues with your boundaries now.

You need to speak what you need and then enforce that you will not tolerate less.

This whole process is designed to kill your people pleaser. Oh, that darned people pleaser we all must battle. You have spent way, way, *way* too much time ensuring that those around you are pleased and happy. That is not the goal of your life. You do not exist to make other people happy. I repeat, you do not exist to make other people happy. Not only is that not your job, but you literally never ever will succeed. Because it is impossible. If you or anyone else's happiness relies on someone else, you will always 100 percent be disappointed. Because we are all human and we all exist in our own ways.

In our society, we have been told that it is actually not good to make others unhappy, and your abuser reinforced that. So by setting boundaries, clear concise boundaries, with your partner, you are rewiring your mind to understand that serving your own needs is not selfish, but rather what you need in order to be healthy. We will work more with the Wound Triggers you have with this in the next chapter, but I wanted to be sure that you go into these boundaries conversations knowing that you deserve to have them and that the whole world will not fall apart if you ask your partner to respect them. It won't. I know you may be afraid that it will, but it won't. I promise.

To communicate your boundaries, you need to try to avoid talking about the situation that you wrote about. You will want to talk about it. You will want to bring it up to prove your need.

You will *really want to talk about it.* This comes from a wound where you believe that in order for anyone to respect you, you must prove your worthiness. You are worthy inherently. You don't have to prove it to anyone. And if you bring up the situation, you will lose your point. Don't bring it up. Just put it away. Leave it alone. The situation is a story, and stories make people rather feely. And if you bring up the story, the feels that your partner has around it often won't mirror your own, and that will literally make his ears shut off. No, when talking about your boundary needs with your partner, you want to make sure that you are not currently in a place where your boundaries are being violated (not for the initial conversation at least), and that you are calm and not triggered. Then you want to lead with your Boundary Statement. You want to tell your partner that it is important to you to feel X. That it is a need of yours. Make it clear that you are not accusing him of anything at the present moment, but that you have noticed this is a need that is feeling overlooked, and that you need his support in helping you feel this need is met.

It is important that this conversation does not go to a place of accusations. Boundaries are inherently triggering for both the establisher and the receiver. You will be triggered by having to communicate a boundary, and it is not rare for your partner to be triggered by hearing a boundary, because, well basically, it is human nature to take things personally. Which is why it is so essential when establishing a boundary that you focus the conversation on your need, not on all the ways in which you feel your partner is not respecting that need.

Keeping this focus will help you communicate clearly and will help you be able to then enforce the boundary later on.

If, say, a month later, your partner, or other person that you have communicated your boundary with, crosses your boundary, you now have the verbiage and background to let them know that they have just done so. No one *has* to respect your boundaries, but you need to be clear that in order to be in your life they *must* respect them. If your boundary is crossed, you want to tell your partner using your Boundary Statement and the current situation. Not in an accusatory way that attacks his *why* for crossing the boundary, but rather in a way that lets him know that what he is doing is crossing your boundary and you need him to respect that this is not acceptable and reiterate what you need. This can be hard, but sometimes it requires repetition to maintain and fully establish your boundary.

It is also important that you continue to enforce your boundaries with yourself. Don't let anyone cross your boundaries without you speaking to them about it. If you don't act on your boundaries, then you are allowing yourself to be uncomfortable, because it makes someone else feel better, and you owe it to yourself to not force yourself into discomfort out of any sort of fear. Your monster should not be given that power. Ever.

---

*The wizard leads you through the forest, humming a merry tune as he goes. He hasn't said anything since you told him off. And as you tromp through the underbrush, you begin to feel the pings of nervousness tickling at the edge of your thoughts. Is he leading you away because he doesn't want you as a pupil anymore? Is he angry? Where the blazes are you going? Finally, you get to a clearing filled with large boulders of all different sorts. There are ones that gleam brightly with gold, silver, and bronze and those that are dark and deep and look as if they would take a hundred men to move. There are small ones and large ones and ones of brilliant greens and purples. They are beautiful. The wizard grabs your hand and lifts it up so your palm is facing the boulders.*

*"Repeat after me," he says. "I seek protection, not because I cannot protect myself, but rather because I can."*

*As you say the words, you feel a power within you and energy springing from your very soul exploding outward from the meat of your palm. You hear a rumbling from within the collection of boulders. Your hand gleams with gold, a magnetic heat you cannot describe, and slowly you see a boulder rise from the pile. It climbs skyward, molding itself into a new form. Disconnecting into differ-*

*ent segments and parts, twisting and smoothing all the while. Then, with a whoosh of air, it comes to you. The pieces settle themselves on your arms and legs, your breast and back and stomach. The stone wraps around you, protecting your limbs, fortifying your defenses. It clings to you, bracing you against the world. You are surprised; despite it being forged from stone, it is light, easy to move in. Slowly you open and close your hands and throw your arms about, examining the brilliance of the trophy you have just grasped.*

---

Congratulations, you have earned your armor! A heavy suit of boundaries is your protection. They are your ability to defend yourself from creating more trauma in your life by sacrificing your needs for other people's wants of you. Relationships are all about balance, and with anything, there will be give and take, but now you have the tool to help you focus on your healing. Your growth and purpose and happiness.

Fun-part time. You get to decide what your character's armor looks like! Decorate it up! Does it have a pattern? Is it a shining silver armor, or a heavy steel armor? Maybe it's thick elfin leather! It's up to you, but create the armor for your character however you see fit and make sure that it matches the character of you! Be proud – I am sure your character is seriously starting to look like a warrior.

# Level 7:

# Dig for the Roots of Hurt.
# Re-Understanding Trauma

"It is time," the wizard says. He gingerly wraps up the remnants of last night's dinner for you in a piece of cloth. You take the food from him, tucking it into your bag. You are moving forward on the next step of your journey. He has told you to go north to the mountains where you will find the mountain warriors. They will teach you what you need to fight the *beast. He has taught you all he can – after all, he is a peaceful being. Concerned with preservation and protection, it is not his place to teach true combat. He has shown you your magic and created the space for you to get your armor and shield, but weapons, those are not in his repertoire. You must adventure on.*

---

Congratulations! Your character is officially halfway to the XP needed to take on the beast. You are sitting at a Level 6 and actively approaching a Level 7!

Now that we have discussed Boundary Triggers at length, we need to start moving onto the Wound Triggers. However, in order to fully be able to dive in, it is important that you understand what trauma is.

Trauma is an experience *or program* that has caused you pain or hardship in the past. I am sure that this is as familiar a concept to you as it is to everyone, but the way that I want you to understand trauma actually goes much beyond this. By going very, very small.

We have a habit, as a species, to define our lives by the things we overcame. I am not saying that this is inherently a bad thing; however, it does make the story of your life tend to revolve around some of your largest traumas, and therefore you start to think of those experiences as the key ones that defined you. When, in fact, most of the trauma that has occurred in your mind and to your spirit actually happened in super tiny, micro doses.

Here is what I mean.

I have *amazing* parents. They are wonderful and loving and completely supportive of everything I ever want to do. Growing up, they pushed me to follow my dreams and reinforced that I could be anything that I wanted. That I could do anything that I wanted. That I had the power to choose my life. And I worked really, really hard at my dreams. Like, really hard. I took *all* advanced placement classes and even took extra classes that I didn't need to take. I love knowledge, and I wanted to figure out exactly what I wanted to do before I entered college. I am aware that this plan would have probably backfired, but in my high school mind, it was the best thing ever. When I finally landed on what I wanted to do (humanities and history), I searched high and low for the school I wanted to attend. And I found one! I wanted to go so badly. They had their own humanities department *and* were located in my favorite city of all time! I mean, so perfect, right? Well, I rushed in to tell my dad that I had found it, the school that I wanted to go to! I was so ready and so excited and I expected him to be, too. But that is not the reaction I got. In fact, I got the opposite reaction. He told me I couldn't go to that school, that I couldn't even apply. And I didn't understand. I was hurt, crushed, and more than anything, and something I didn't realize at the time, I started to question why I was even trying if I couldn't, in fact, do everything I wanted. If I couldn't be everything that I wanted to be. I was discouraged from even trying because it was going to be a no.

Don't get me wrong, looking back at it I completely see where my dad was coming from. The school I wanted to go to was really, really expensive (something so trivial in my high school mind) and my parents had already prepaid much of my tuition to a different, closer, less-expensive school. Which was still a really good school, just not my dream school. It was my first dose of real life, and I didn't take it great.

I didn't realize until *much* later how that little dose of life actually was traumatic for me. I have had far more traumatic things happen to me since then, so on the surface it seemed so small. But I was discrediting the powerless feeling I took from that experience that then carried over to my later years and since then have spent copious amounts of time diving into, dissecting, and healing from.

My parents were only looking out for what was best for me. But, because of my nature and already existing beliefs and programs, this was traumatic for me.

It is easy to judge this experience as trivial even still because the actual event was small, but the feelings were big. Very big. Even if it took me quite a long time to understand that.

As you think about your life, notice *how* you think about it. Do you define your life story by the bad things or the good? Is that how you want to define your story? Neither way is wrong, but you should be making the conscious choice of how you want to describe your existence. I have joked that I can tell my life story three ways, by everything that happened (storybook style), how I felt about everything (biography version), and why everything happened (the magic version). And how I tell the story is based on the listener, but how I think of my story, that is based on me.

When you think of your trauma, you must come at it with an open mind, totally receptive to whatever trauma and wound comes up. And if something that seems small pops up, don't dismiss it. You are doing no one any favors by downplaying your feelings, whether they are current feelings or ones that occurred long ago. If you judge your trauma, you rob yourself of your ability to heal it. Traumatic experiences are not a peeing contest. In fact, people who have experienced a lot of trauma in their lives tend to instantly tell you that they don't have it as bad as some people, or at least "blank" didn't happened to them. Don't do this to yourself.

I have a secret for you…you have been brainwashed. Time and time again, over and over again, to think that your problems aren't as real as other people's problems. Anything that caused hardship for you in your life, no matter how tiny, is real. It is real to you. And you are the only person that it needs to be real for. Your experiences are yours, allow yourself to be honest in understanding that some trauma may seem silly or that, to your logical mind, you should not have taken it so seriously or better understood the situation. But none of what your logical mind says to you about it matters. It was traumatic to you for a reason. You are allowed to heal even the little things.

Here is a super duper "silly" example of this from my own life. I had braces in middle school, and not the fun invisible ones they have now, but the painful metal ones with…head-gear. Yup, I was mega popular. Pair that with the fact that I was five foot nine inches in the sixth grade; it all made me a really approachable person. Anyway, I digress. I was, and still am, a huge *Survivor* fan. I begged my mom for a coconut. One day she got one from the store. My plan for cracking the coconut open was to use a flat-head screwdriver and a hammer outside on the patio. I hammered away for a good hour before I could finally get it to break open. I was pumped until I noticed that the inside was brown and rotten, the whole thing. I was pissed. Well, I was sad, but I acted pissed. I even tried to make it funny by throwing a "fake" tantrum on the living room floor to cover up my disappointment. This is my first real memory of burying my own feelings for the comfort of others. But, in the heat of my "fake" tantrum, my braces got stuck to the carpet. Like, really, really stuck. My mom had to help me with scissors amount of stuck. We still joke about the braces and the carpet fairly often. And it's a funny memory! But also wouldn't have happened if I hadn't traumatized myself into thinking that I couldn't just share my feelings. I literally got my braces stuck to the carpet. And the story keeps coming up. As soon as you notice your patterns and stories, you will be able to see this in your life, too.

Don't get me wrong, it's a hilarious story. But it's also a fabulous example of the nature of trauma, where the feeling and the story are two very different things.

Also, if you were reading close enough, you may have identified my lovely people pleaser rear her head. We mentioned your people pleaser briefly last chapter, but now I want you to really think about all the times in your life when you have either allowed yourself to be traumatized or traumatized yourself because you were being a people pleaser. Once you start to think about it, you will be astonished at the amount of times that this has happened. It is amazing to want to help others, but it should not be at the cost of sacrificing yourself.

When I was young, my mother worked part-time for the author Leo Buscaglia. He wrote and spoke about love in ways that affected millions of people, but to me he was just Uncle Leo. I have a few very strong memories of him, but one I will never forget is once when he was reading to me. We were in his yellow office with the walls lined with books and the floor covered in a shag throw carpet. Most of the books on the walls were boring to me and had no pictures, yuck, right? But I had brought some from home. One of which was *The Giving Tree*, by Shel Silverstein. When he saw it, he asked me if I knew that story, and I, maybe five years old, said yes I did and that I liked it. He then told me he didn't like the story of *The Giving Tree*. I asked him why. I remember being confused by this even then, because he was usually all about helping others. And he told me that we should never give anyone all of ourselves, because that will never make anyone happy. Truly helping people does not require that you give all that you are, but rather that you give it your all.

That has always stuck with me, and as an adult thinking on that story, it is literally the biggest people pleaser warning ever. The tree gives *everything* it has to the boy and never ever is the boy satisfied. But the tree only values itself when it is giving to the boy. If you take away one thing from this book, I hope it is the notion that being the Giving Tree will never fulfill you and will do nothing but re-traumatize your life over and over again.

Now that you can acknowledge where your traumas can come from, we get to move on to the best part of your adventure: the final preparations to take on your Fear Monster. You are going to heal your trauma.

---

*You embrace the wizard warmly, thankful for all he has shown you and eager to start on the next part of your journey. He wishes you well and you set off. You are a good week's hike from the mountains, giving you plenty of time to think and practice your magic as you go. You had thought that you would be sad to leave the wizard, but you don't feel sad, you feel thankful. Thankful for all he has taught you, even though it was difficult. Thankful that you feel thankful. That you get to progress on this journey. That you don't feel the need to look back at the little house in the clearing, as all he's taught you gives you the courage instead to look forward.*

---

# Cut Through Your Pain and Heal Yourself for Good

*he wind is howling in your ears as you gingerly find your footing on the rocky mountain path. It's steep. Very steep. You are thankful when you breach the side of a level plateau. You see it in front of you. The purpose of your trek. There are caves, a great many of them, bore deep into the side of the mountain. People sit in front of them, and smoke wafts from their openings carrying the smell of food. This is the first time you have ever been this far from your village. Days and days from your village. They see you approaching, and a few of them rise to greet you. You start to introduce yourself, but one of them, a strong woman wearing heavy leather clothing, cuts you off. They already know who you are. The wizard sent them a raven, and they have been expecting you.*

*She shows you into a cave. It smells musty and dark, and it takes a moment for your eyes to adjust. She leads to a bedroll they have laid out for you and hands you some food. She tells you to rest, for there will be little of that in the coming days. You get the feeling that this training is going to be quite unlike that which you received from the wizard.*

---

Now that you can identify your trauma and have a broader understanding of what trauma is, it is time that we tackle it head-on. The first thing that you must do when tackling your trauma is be consciously aware of when your wounds pop up, and own that it is *your* wound. It is easy to blame others, specifically our partners, when we are intensely triggered, but that is never ever going to help in the healing process.

The biggest magic in this process is your ability to understand that your trauma is yours, and how you react to it is yours as well. You will be looking inward and working on you, with you helping.

At this point you may be like, "What?" I promise it will make sense in a second.

In order for me to explain this process fully, I want to be sure that you understand how I discovered it. You may have heard people speak about your inner child. The inner child is a way of connecting you with your authentic self, and when I first started on my healing journey, I was taught an inner-child tool. And to be honest, I couldn't understand for the longest time why it wasn't working for me. The idea behind it was this: when you got triggered, first of all, you needed to talk to what was dubbed a gremlin, essentially the part of you that was feeling triggered, and tell that gremlin that he needed to go away. And then you needed to mentally talk to your inner child as if you were talking to your daughter or son, and counsel them through whatever pain they were feeling. Now, don't get me wrong, this definitely works for some people, but this 100 percent didn't work for me.

There were some crucial problems with this method for me. Problem one: telling the gremlin to basically die did not align with me at all. Like, where the heck is he going to go? Nowhere. That felt wholly like bypassing in a very unhealthy way. Problem two: the main trauma that I had gone through didn't happen to me as a child. Sure, we all have childhood trauma, some much larger than others, but this method in no way helped me to heal the wounds that occurred in me from when I was in an abusive relationship.

So I came up with a new way. A way that not only worked for me, but that I have seen work for many clients, and that I know is incredibly powerful and can heal your wounds for good.

In order to use this tool, you will need to get comfortable visualizing yourself talking to yourself. And this may require some practice. It may feel clunky at first or could come to you easily, but whatever happens, understand that you are learning. Visualization is a skill, and you may need to practice it in order for it come easily to you. However, even if it's clunky, this tool will still be just as powerful.

When you are triggered, and you identify it as a Wound Trigger, I recommend starting with the heavy triggers, aka the ones that are very easy for you to identify because they are associated with very strong emotions. The very first thing that you need to do is acknowledge it. Basically say, either in your head or out loud, "I am triggered by _____." This is where the emotional intelligence work that you did earlier will come in handy.

Next, after you have acknowledged your trigger, you need to take a moment to sit somewhere and close your eyes. This can be done right where you are standing, or by you running to your bedroom or excusing yourself to the bathroom, wherever you can comfortably have a moment. I encourage you to, if you're triggered by something that is occurring in your relationship, state that you are triggered and need a moment to your partner, keeping that open communication line flowing, and then step away.

What you want to try and avoid at this point in time is falling into the emotion you are feeling. As discussed earlier, you will typically be feeling a very dense emotion that is easy to get caught up in. That is why saying the "I am triggered" statement above will really help you. It makes your brain stop for a moment and not get swept up in the emotion. You will still be feeling the emotion, but this will help you to not get completely overwhelmed by it. Basically, it stops you from taking a full shot of emotion hormones that can cloud your vision.

When you are alone, close your eyes and think about your trigger. Ask yourself, "When do I remember feeling what I am feeling now the most intensely?" Depending on the trigger, you may have a very clear answer to this already in mind before you even close your eyes, but sometimes, especially when your mind has placed blocks on your memory for your protection, the answer may not come as easily. But do your best to try and remember at least one time in your past where you felt intensely the same as you do in the moment of the trigger. However, if you can't remember a specific time, just think of yourself younger in your mind.

When you have a memory or time in your life identified, you need to picture yourself as you were then. Picture how old you were; put yourself in those clothes if you can. Where were you? Were you crying? What were you doing?

Look at yourself in your mind's eye, and as clearly as you can, tell yourself what you wished someone would have said to you then. Tell yourself that you love you, that what he was doing is not okay, that you have a right to be safe, that it is okay to cry, to feel broken, that you understand you were just trying to survive. Whatever feels right to you, tell yourself that. Give yourself a hug if that's what comes to mind, but the most important part is trust yourself. Trust that whatever comes up for you to say is what you need to say.

This can be hard and emotional, it can bring up pain, but in order to heal our wounds, we must allow them to be felt.

If the past you has something to say back to you, let her say it. Hear her out, give her all the understanding that you *wish you had then*. Love her the way you wish someone would have loved you then.

There are no specific guidelines for how long you should be consoling yourself, but you will know when you are done. When you have said all you needed to, and you feel heard. It will feel like closure.

Sometimes it's difficult to visualize your past you, or you can't lock in a specific memory. If you are experiencing that, it can help to create a calm place for you to speak with your past selves and put your conversations there. When you find your wounded self, before talking with her, picture her and you in your place. Together there and peaceful, tell her that it is a safe place. This can help your mind believe that as well and can ease your subconscious into being more comfortable with visualizing your wounded you.

By doing this work, you are literally healing the wounds and reframing the way your mind thinks about specific traumas to no longer make them painful, but rather just memories.

Now, it may take more than one time speaking to yourself for a wound to be healed. The bigger the wound, the more time, but that is all part of the process. And you will notice that after each time you speak to yourself, that trigger will get less and less, and the conversations will get easier and easier.

Notice that I call these talks conversations. You have to let your past you speak back, or you will be in resistance and will find it very difficult to heal what you need to.

Another way that you can work through your Trauma Wounds is through letter writing. This method can be really helpful if you didn't stop your brain with your "I am triggered" statement in time and end up in full-blown anxiety attack mode. When you are in anxiety, it is nearly impossible to visualize, and that is all right. This method not only helps you calm down but also helps you begin to heal and gets you to a place where you can visualize.

For this, you will need, you guessed it, your journal (and pen of awesome). If you are experiencing an anxiety attack, I want you to sit down and write a letter. This letter you will write to a friend, or a fellow character, or you can write to the wizard if it helps or someone else that you have created in your game that is helping you on your journey, or even your mom. But whoever you are writing to, address the letter to them. And then you are going to write to them about the anxiety or trigger that *they* are feeling. Talk to them as if they are the one feeling everything that you are in the current moment. Tell them that they are okay, and you know how it is to feel powerless and out of control. Be sure you are talking *to them*. Picture them, imagine that they are feeling what you are, and help them through it. Tell them that you care.

Don't judge what you write in any way; just write and write and write, until you are feeling better. Until you feel that you have told them what they need to hear. Until you feel it's time to sign the letter. And then end the letter by saying something like you are there if they need you, and then love and your name. Leave it open ended, leave room for further conversation.

And then after you have written your letter, do what you need to help you move any remaining emotions that you are feeling. Dance, take a shower, sing at the top of your lungs, scroll through social media, whatever is fine.

Then, the next day or later that night if you are feeling up to it, reread your letter. Hold on to it. It is nice to have the letter to read again if you need to. If you get to that point again, it can help to read the letter back to yourself. And it will help you start to better identify when you begin to get triggered over time.

The most important part of using either of the above tools is to not judge yourself. However you are feeling, whatever trauma may come up, *all* of it is valid. All of it is *real*. No one gets to tell you it's not. If it is pain, then it is pain. Period.

Also, remember it may be hard at first, but you are not doing it wrong. It takes practice, and not only that, it takes repetition to get full healing on wounds. And that is all perfectly fine. As long as you are doing the work, you will push through.

These tools are game changers for your life and relationship. Be sure to talk to your partner about what you are doing and going through. Being transparent with others will help you to be transparent with yourself; however, be sure to lay down the boundary that they do not get to judge you, either, and that their opinion on your trauma is not wanted or necessary; you just want to share with them what you are experiencing. You can even tell them that you just want them to say that they see you and give you a hug once you are done sharing.

The reason for this is that you need to make sure that you are feeling safe while you share so you don't re-traumatize yourself during your process of healing.

———————————————

*The woman wasn't lying when she told you that you would need rest. In the days following your arrival to the mountain village you began a rigorous training regimen. Wake, eat, train, sleep. She would take you to the side of the mountain and have you lift and move boulders until your arms ached and fingers were red with blood, then instruct you to put them all back again. She was strengthening you, causing your muscles to grow and expand.*

*"To take on the beast, you must be strong," she would say.*

*Then, once you were exhausted, you would spend time in the ring with your shield and a tiny wooden sword, learning to block and pivot and strike.*

*"To take on the beast, you must be agile," she would say, "and you must have skill, you must learn to see how warriors see."*

*At night, all the village people would tell stories around the fire, of other monsters, battles long ago fought. You would listen closely and try with all your might to commit the stories to memory, so that when you took on the beast you would be able to use their strategies. To channel their wisdom.*

*One day, she tells you to climb the mountain. You look at her, fear and confusion on your face, standing in front of a jagged wall of rock and mud. "Climb," she says again. And you do. You strap your shield to your back and fight your way up, digging your fingers into crevices and toes onto ledges. She is behind you, encouraging you, driving you onward. You don't know how long you climb, as you force your mind to stay present, focused on the task at hand. Finally, there is a ledge large enough to stand on, and you hoist yourself onto it, panting and muddy. The wind is strong here. You hear her climb on behind you and drop something onto the ground by your head. You roll to look at it. A sword. Metal and heavy, glistens there. You grasp it in your hand and stand. It is not so heavy as it would have been back in your village. "Fight," she says and draws her weapon. For a moment you want to hesitate, but instead swing, hard and fast, and block with your shield. It is a dance, her sword then yours, your feet then hers, moving and focused on each other, on the ledge. Finally, with a delicate movement you back her to the ledge angling your blade to her. She smiles; you have seen.*

---

Congratulations, you have leveled up and gained your ever-coveted sword! Whoop, whoop, weapon time! Take pride in this. Be sure to give your character a sword and know that it is a tool as much as it is a weapon. It is the crucial piece that gets you one step closer to facing your beast head-on and coming out victorious.

# Allow Your Tears to Launch
# You Forward

*fter receiving your sword, the days pass quickly, the training no longer so daunting as your body and mind strengthen. You begin to think of it all as a game, you against you, pushing yourself to improve. The woman has said there is one last thing you need before you can take on the beast. You must learn to shoot. For this, she says, it is not simply a matter of practice, but also one of cen-*

*tering. You cannot aim if your vision is clouded by anger or regret. You must release what you have long kept protected. It is the only way. She brings you to an open field near the top of the mountain with targets lined up in neat rows. Already waiting at the field is a man, large in build but also graceful in his movements. As you approach him, she introduces you. He looks down at you but seems to stare through you. You try not to gasp as you realize it is because his eyes see nothing at all.*

---

This chapter is not so much a tool, but a permission. I am hereby giving you permission to be. To be exactly what you are as you are now. I love you. I see you. And now it is time that you see yourself.

Before you dated your abuser, you were someone else. You had different dreams, and a different reality. Not only did you see the world in a different way than you do now, but people saw you in a different way than they do now.

Who you are now is not a worse version of who you were then, and who you were then is not a worse version of what you are now. All the ways that you have existed have been the ways you were meant to be in that time. And it is my sincerest hope that, through this game, you can see this truth.

However, now you must do something that you most likely have not done before. You need to grieve. Too often as humans, we move from one part of our life to the next without acknowledging who we were and what we lost. The easiest example of this is when someone has a baby. Society has a completely unreasonable standard that we should feel a certain way after we have a baby. That our life is complete and wonderful by their presence. And don't get me wrong, being a mother is incredibly fulfilling. But I remember the day I found out I was pregnant for the first time and thinking, *Nothing will ever be the same again*. And though that is not a bad thing, we do ourselves a disservice by not allowing ourselves to grieve who we were that we left behind.

So now is your time. Find some time to sit by yourself or to talk with a friend and grieve yourself. Grieve the naivety that you once had. The innocence and faith in people that was taken from you. Grieve the person that you once were, the one who didn't think it could happen to her, the one who was free and un-hardened by the world, who believed in love with all her heart. And grieve not only her, but what she lost. Grieve for the dreams that can no longer be that you once held so dear. Cry for those dreams. It is okay to feel loss. It is okay to be sad about it.

You don't need to be strong to be strong.

Let yourself be sad, but don't pity yourself. You are not worse because you lost. You are stronger and more caring, and you sure as all heck are not broken.

If you are scared of being overwhelmed by your sadness, that is fine. Set a timer, a half hour of sad, and then go do something physical. Dance or go for a walk. Find a dog and hug it. But go do something. And set yourself another half an hour on a different day.

This process can take however long you feel it needs to, but I promise, when paired with the other tools we have discussed, you will find the closure you may not even know you needed.

It may feel very uncomfortable to allow yourself this space to feel, but it is so incredibly necessary. This is the act of holding space for yourself. Of honoring yourself. It is easy to push our sadness down because we want to move on, to move forward, but you cannot be who you are becoming without loving who you once were and letting her go. You are learning to be comfortable in your grief, to not judge it, and to embrace its life-changing power. Allowing yourself to grieve allows yourself to grow.

The next part of this is forgiveness. And I am *not* at all talking about forgiving your abuser, though you may find in time that you do naturally as you heal your wounds and step into your power. No, I am talking about forgiving yourself. No one ever goes into a relationship knowing that it will be abusive. It creeps up on you through the days and weeks until you are in it fully. Until you are trapped. This is how abuse destroys your sense of self first. Because you found yourself in abuse, you immediately doubt yourself. It creates a world of no longer being able to trust yourself as you once did.

But let me clear this up right now, you didn't do anything wrong, you didn't make a mistake. You did what you had to do to survive. Everything that you went through is not your fault.

When you read that, your mind probably said something like, *You don't know that*, or *But I was the one who made the decision to stay*, or any number of things to dismiss you. And that is how I know you need to hear it.

Everything that you went through was not your fault.

You must allow yourself to forgive yourself. Forgive the staying and the yelling and the fighting. Forgive yourself for hurting those around you in an effort to protect your abuser and therefore yourself. Forgive yourself for the jobs or the friends you lost. Forgive yourself of every mistake you feel like you made. And then remember, it was not your fault. You were a victim, but you aren't any longer.

You made it through; you are here. And yes, there will be those who don't understand what you did, but you don't need anyone else's forgiveness to free yourself from your guilt. Forgive yourself by telling yourself that you are sorry and then telling yourself you forgive yourself.

Look in the mirror after you brush your teeth each night, and forgive yourself for something. Every night. Tell yourself you forgive yourself for something. And mean it. You may have to forgive the same thing more than once, but don't let that stop you. Forgive yourself over and over again. Because you are worthy of forgiveness.

———————————

*You are surprised by how much the man can see with no eyesight. He knows when your elbow is too low or when your legs are too close together by the sound of the wind flying off your arrow, the twang of your bow string. He tells you to arch your back and deepen your breathing while leaning his ear toward you. You shoot arrow after arrow but stick very few into even the very closest targets. "Be patient with yourself," he says. "You cannot expect to hit a target without a steady soul." Put your pain to the wind, with each nock of an arrow and each pull of the string, whisper your pain to the feathers and let it fly. "An arrow cannot fly without being pulled backward," he says as he pulls your arm. "Don't hate it for having it be so."*

*Day after day, you shoot. Over and over. You make progress, not as much as you would like at first, and then gradually more and more until you can hit the closest targets easily. He makes you run and shoot. And jump and shoot. Then one day he covers your eyes as his are. You learn to listen, to trust. And for the first time, you notice that the fire within you, the one that has burned for so long for the beast's destruction, doesn't hurt as much as it once did. Its flames no longer lap at the corners of your consciousness. You no longer can picture the smoldering remnants of your house with fury flooding your veins.*

*And then one day, you feel it. An easiness within you like the smooth glass surface of a lake. You are ready. You are ready to take on the beast. This battle will end once and for all. Your teacher can feel it, too. He takes you to the forest and instructs you in the wood to cut and how to prepare it. Then how to carve and strengthen it until it bends in the way you need it to. Then the strength it takes to string it to make it operable.*

*You fight with it awhile until the string locks on. He hears it and smiles. "It is time you complete your quest," he says.*

———————————

You have earned your bow and arrows. And with each dream you grieve, and mistake you forgive, you will be able to shoot it more and more clearly. You are propelling yourself forward toward your future healthy state. Be sure you give your character a fitting bow and decorative arrows. This is the final preparation. You are about to take on your Fear Monster. You are ready.

Level 10:

# The Final Battle, Overcome

Y ou are ready. More ready than you have ever dreamed you could be. But that doesn't make you not afraid. You smile to yourself. You used to think that, with all the training you did, you wouldn't be afraid. You would have the utmost confidence in yourself to take on the beast. That your anger and the creature would propel you forward. But as you hide in the bushes staring at the gaping cracked cavern that the beast inhabits, it is not so. You are afraid, but that is all right with you somehow. It would

101

*feel wrong if you felt no fear. As if you took what you are about to do too lightly.*

*Calmly, you nock an arrow and aim at the cavern, inhaling sharply and releasing it toward the darkness. It flies through the opening and clatters against the rock inside. You hear stirring from within the blackness and nock another arrow, this time standing above the bush and straining your eyes to get your first glimpse of the beast as it emerges.*

*Scraping of claw against rock and moving of heavy limbs mixed with pant of thick breath. You let your arrow fly at the first glint of shiny scale. You hear it scatter off the monster's thick hide. A hiss passes your lips in frustration. You slide your arm into your shield and draw your sword as the beast takes its first step into the light.*

*It stretches its wings out and rears onto its hind legs. It's massive, much larger than you ever could have thought. You have only ever seen it from a distance, and it is as if your memory shrunk it to be more palatable. This is the first time you have seen it up close. For a moment it takes your breath away – not out of fear, but out of awe. It is beautiful. Its colorful hide catches the light and sends rainbows dancing out in all directions. Its body moves with graceful ease despite its size, its tail waves behind it smoothly, as if a flame flickering from a candle. Most striking are its eyes. They are large and smooth and clear as glass, and you see yourself reflected in those eyes as the beast stares down at you. You are lost in those eyes for a moment. Those orbs of light beaming down onto you. They are real, raw, deep eyes. Eyes that have seen thousands of years and know thousands of wisdoms. They are not the eyes of a killer.*

*You realize that the beast is not attacking you. Rather, it is studying you. Waiting, watching. It seems to know you. To know your pain and your anger, but it doesn't hate you for it. Your eyes fall to its stomach. There are scars there from those who tried before you to slay the beast.*

*You finally understand. It is not a beast for slaying. To slay it would be an impossibility. But to understand it…that is something you can achieve.*

---

You may have seen this coming. But let's be honest, the visual is powerful. Your Fear Monster is not the enemy. In fact, by simply following the previous steps, you have already tamed this beast. If the reason you haven't yet is because you have been waiting in anticipation of this chapter, well, go for it. Use your tools and heal your wounds.

It is important to understand that, with this process, we are not trying to *get rid* of fear. You can never not be afraid – that is not healthy. If you lost that guide to your wounds, you would never be able to heal them. No, your goal is to heal your trauma so that you can free yourself from unnecessary pain.

The goal is to stop abusing yourself.

Yes, your abuser gave you the trauma, but it is you that have held it. You may have even relied on it as a part of your identity or as a way of bypassing. But now it is time to understand it and move on from it.

You cannot defeat the Fear Monster, but you don't have to be afraid of it. You can ride it. You have the power, and I will tell you one more secret: the best way to free yourself from all the abuse and trauma you have ever suffered is to simply be you.

Be so authentically and unapologetically you that you take back all the power that you gave away. I know that this can be harder than it sounds, but start small and work your way up. Tell your partner what you want for dinner, or that you don't like when he randomly grabs your butt. Have a night out with your girlfriends and don't apologize for it. Or, better yet, don't apologize when your partner does something to take care of you. You are not a burden; you don't owe anyone anything for loving you. You will have wounds to heal around this, but you are enough.

That's it, the last step in the process – you tame the beast by allowing yourself to be freely you. You have the tools, and with each step forward, your love for you will grow a bit more and, with that, so will your life.

And there is even more magic in that than you can imagine. For with each wound you heal, you open yourself up to the Universe. You free yourself from blocks and you can work with the

Universe to manifest the life you have always wanted. Remember when you wrote that letter? Well, the more you use the tools, not only will all the things in the letter come true, but you have the power to cocreate with the universe at will. You will be able to manifest your dreams easily. You have the power. There is no limit to your growth potential.

---

*You throw your sword and shield to the ground. The beast cocks its head to one side. You take a few steps forward, approaching it cautiously, still gazing at its powerful eyes. Slowly it lowers its head a bit, inspecting you intensely. You are not afraid. You understand now; it is not the beast's fault that you didn't listen when it warned you to build your house somewhere else. You didn't listen when you invaded its space. You didn't listen. Its goal was not to harm you, but to live. Its head drops farther until you are eye to massive, translucent eye. There is peace here and understanding that you never thought possible.*

*You reach your hand out and lay it gently on the beast's nose. It is smooth. You smile. It was not the beast you needed to conquer; it was the journey.*

---

Now for the fun part – keep your character going! Decorate the crap out of it, give your character a pet, make new Fear Monsters as you tackle more of your wounds – anything that keeps you physically focused on your healing. I still have monsters that I create that I am working through, and that is okay. Some of our wounds are meant to take awhile to heal. Putting them in monster form helps to make them not as daunting, as strange as that sounds. The thing that makes this process so successful is the physical representation that we create to push ourselves forward. In the thinking of yourself as a character, you are able to view your monsters in a new way and reframe your story. Just be you. Don't take yourself too seriously, and keep making the whole process a game. It is a game, and you are learning about you, and that is fun.

# No Adventure Is Worth
# Having Alone

ell, there it is, the game of curing your anxiety. I
hope that ending wasn't too much of a surprise, and
that you enjoyed the journey, learning more about
yourself in the process.

It has meant the world to me that I have gotten to share
in your adventure. I wrote this book because I want to help
people reclaim what they lost in abuse. I want to empower
you and all people to have healthy relationships. But also, to

remind everyone of the power of play.

There is one last secret ingredient in this process that makes the results even more potent and invaluable. That is the power of community. No good game should ever have only one character, and it is through community that we build each other up. And we create new stories for our characters.

You may be thinking, *Yes, this all looks good on paper and I am totally going to do it!* And to that I say, "Heck yeah!" Please, let me help you. It can be daunting to embark on such a quest solo. In fact, though it is still possible to be successful without it, if you have a community backing you and someone to help guide you and hold you through the tough parts, it eliminates the option of failure. One of the main things that I do while supporting my clients is help them bust through their road-blocks, the things that stop them from progressing forward. It is easy to get caught up in the whirlwind of life, swept up in the day to day and blown about by your feelings, and to be honest, even with all the tools in the world, sometimes it's just dang hard to see the root of your trauma. It is my goal to keep you not only focused, but to help guide you to the root of what is causing your blocks, to help you navigate your resistance. I help my clients by being the mirror that they need in order for them to better see their trauma and what needs to be done to work through it.

Let's be honest, it is so wonderful to know you have a completely nonjudgmental, unbiased (well once you work with me, I am biased in your favor because I love my clients) person to bounce all your ick off of, especially when it comes to the sensitive parts of the healing process. I am very aware that some of your trauma will feel painfully raw to acknowledge, and I am equipped and ready to support you. And, especially when dealing with fears, it can be easy and more comfortable to run and hide from them, particularly when you find a truly scary one. But when you have support, all those fears seem less terrifying and therefore are far easier to address head-on.

What I am trying to say is, yes, you can use this process very successfully on your own with just this guide, but if you harness the power of a team and coach that knows this game inside and out, you can get deeper and much more meaningful results in a far shorter and more enjoyable amount of time.

On top of that, you definitely don't want to put all that time and effort into your character and Fear Monster and not get to share it with people who understand. I want to revel in your creativity! To raise you up to new heights and see the genius that is hiding in the inner workings of your mind. I strongly believe that creative expression is one of the most powerful ways to heal ourselves, and sharing your creativity helps to heal others as well. I want to be able to see your character and

Fear Monster and watch them grow as you do!

I know how important it is to you to overcome your relationship anxiety. I know the pain that it is causing you, and I know what is at stake if you don't. You don't want to be alone, and you don't want to feel broken any longer. You don't want to lose your relationship or get stuck in a cycle of attracting only people that will trigger you over and over forever. Because that is what will happen – when you get triggered into your anxiety, it is the Universe showing you where to heal. And the Universe will just keep sending that trigger your way over and over again until you do the work and release your trauma. Unfortunately, often your triggers don't affect you and you alone, but also your partner. The more you trigger, the more they will, and that doesn't foster the healthy relationship that you deserve to be in.

This game can change all of that. More than anything, I want to play it with you. I want to see your growth and experience your wins. I cannot describe the power of having someone who understands in your court.

For a long time, I wanted to go at it alone. I thought I could heal me. That I would be fine doing it by myself. And for a while, that worked. But then it stopped working. And I didn't understand. I was trying so hard to heal myself and face my pain, why couldn't I get through it? I ended up getting my answer in a very unlikely place – a peer review at my corporate HR job.

In the review, I was called independent to a fault. This blew my mind. *Independent to a fault?* I thought. *What does that even mean?* You see, I had always thought of my independence as a good thing, that it meant that I was strong and valuable. That I was the one in control of ensuring my own success. And on a deeper level, I was afraid, deeply afraid of trusting others.

When my peers gave me that review, they were only referring to my performance at work, but what they didn't see was how that was translating through all aspects of my life without my knowledge of it. I was independent all right, and all that I was showing to my partner over and over again was that I didn't need him. That I could do it myself.

Even in my friendships, I was a great listener. I would hear all their problems out to the fullest, and then when it came time to share mine, I would gloss them over without even realizing I was doing so. I was still being "vulnerable," but just to a level that I deemed was enough to be relatable. It was real, but only partially. I was still remaining protected.

So, when that review sunk in, I went out and joined in on a group coaching program, and for the first time, I shared all the things. The messy and real and sad and raw and the deep things that I barely felt comfortable telling my dog about. I pushed myself, I made the commitment to let others see me and also to let others help me. But not just anyone, people who understood. Who were experiencing similar things to what I was experiencing. And from that, I was able to be truly honest with myself, to truly open up to my partner, and to actually trust again.

I tell that story for a few reasons, the first being to illustrate the power of having not only a guide but a community, and the second to show you the power of trusting again. It wasn't easy, but it was needed.

Sure, I "trusted" myself to do everything all the time.

Sure, I "trusted" my partner not to hurt me.

Sure, I "trusted" that I could overcome my anxiety.

But I never showed up for any of that "trust." I never actually took the action of trust. The Universe is built on action, and if you show up for it, it will always show up for you. That is part of the reason that I have dedicated my life to this coaching. It is deeply important to me to give survivors of abuse a place where they are guaranteed that they will be accepted, where it is 100 percent safe to trust others and be vulnerable. There is such power in that, and I am deeply grateful for the opportunity I have to support that space.

I also learned another important lesson from that review: in order to lead, you must first follow. What I mean by this is that learning with the support of someone who has already fought the battles, already conquered the monsters means that you gain twice the knowledge, both their knowledge of the experience as well as your own.

That is why I started coaching and that is why I wrote this book. I want to help you conquer your beasts and build your kingdom and lead you to the freedom you have always wanted, freedom from your fears. But more than anything, whether with my support or not, I want you to have the relationship that you have always dreamed of. That relationship, the healthy, loving relationship, is completely attainable, and I am so, so happy that you are making it a priority for you. Picking up and reading this book is your first step to achieving that goal, and as I said, the Universe rewards action.

# Objective Achieved!

ongratulations! I am so beyond excited for you from the bottom of my heart. You have done it, you have learned the tools and earned your skills. You now get to begin the epic adventure of using your newfound knowledge to make your world what you wish it to be.

It is my dream for you that you see the power that there is in play. Don't stop playing, ever. Too often, we adults lose ourselves in our self-imposed stress dungeons and forget that our connection through play is part of what makes us human. Enjoy yourself. You have spent far too long pinned down by your Fear

Monsters, but you have the power to free yourself now. Climb on the backs of those monsters and ride them! Tame them and hear their warnings, their amazing lessons.

I want to thank you. It is my greatest honor in life to be able to share my work with the world and see this method help so many. I hope that we get to continue this journey together and help you uncover more and more layers of yourself in the process. I cannot tell you what it means to me to know that you have gotten to play this game. I hope you sincerely enjoyed yourself.

Remember, *you* have the power. No one can ever or will ever take that from you again. You are strong. And you are you, the most amazing and incredibly you there is.

You are the main character in the story, no one else gets to be. It is in your hands to make you happy, to live the life you have always dreamed of, and to find a community, a wonderous group of people who will do nothing but build you up and cheer you on. And a partner that builds you up in a relationship that will never tear you down.

I cannot wait for you to look in the mirror and see the fearless wonder of yourself looking back. Being free from the fear of fear is the most amazing feeling in the world, especially when you have lived in it for so long.

One of my favorite quotes is from Epictetus: "Man is not

worried by real problems so much as by his imagined anxieties about real problems."

Don't imagine your anxieties; you have the power and now the tools to imagine and create something so much greater than that. The rest of your life.

By reading this book, you have taken the first of many steps on the path to your dreams. Don't stand in the way of your own happiness any longer. You see, the good emotions are teachers as well. They teach you to savor the little things and celebrate each day. They teach you the power of a hug and the impact of a smile. Don't forget to honor and feel those emotions just as you do the dense ones, to their absolute guilt-free fullest.

On this quest, you have learned the power of intention. Of viewing yourself as outside of yourself, of understanding what drives you and the magic of your emotions. You learned how to put on a shiny suit of boundaries and, not only that, how to communicate those boundaries in a way that will ensure they are respected. And when you are triggered, you not only can now see how, but also have ways to learn from the trigger. Then to continue on and discover the trauma that is causing the trigger and to heal it, to close the wounds that were cut into your heart long ago. Finally, you learned the power of grief, of honoring who you once were and what you once coveted in order to allow yourself the freedom to move forward, knowing you can still be anyone and anything you want.

It's funny, I don't do well with endings. Whether it be a really good show or a book, endings deeply impact me. I used to avoid them, I would not read the last chapter in something or leave a final episode unwatched. I didn't want it to be over.

This is not over. This story – your story – has just reached its new beginning. Your future is here. It is now. All the best stories start with the ending of another one. That doesn't mean that you forget the lessons that you learned while you were caught in your previous experience, but now you can see those lessons in a totally new light.

So, congratulations on never ignoring your feelings, but instead listening to them to learn where they are leading you. Congratulations for braving the challenges to gain new understanding. Congratulations for no longer being afraid, but rather being motivated. Congratulations for not giving up – not on you or anything you want. Congratulations for not only creating a better relationship with your partner, but a better one with yourself. Congratulations for finally being able to reach the one thing that you have coveted for so long, your own unadulterated and complete freedom.

It takes bravery to tackle this adventure, but don't, not for one moment, think you can't do it, because you can. Absolutely and without a doubt. I believe in you without a slightest hesitation. Trust the process and, most importantly, trust yourself. I promise that you are worthy of it.

And remember: your life is for living. Have fun and enjoy the adventure.

# Thanks for Reading!

As you have completed this book, I know that your commitment to your quest of healing from your abuse and obtaining the healthy relationship of your dreams knows no bounds. While the point of this adventure is to use fun to help you heal, sometimes the journey can be treacherous, and I want to support you as much as possible.

Because of this I have created an exclusive Facebook Group specifically for those brave enough to have completed this journey of healing. This is my personal way of thanking you and giving you further support on your journey by providing you with a safe space to share and support fellow adventurers! It is a private group so everything you share will only be visible by those in the group. You can also share the characters you have created in the group or by tagging me on Instagram @likerofwords. I so desperately want to see them! Join this group by searching Facebook for the group _Be a Damsel No More! Love Again After Abuse._ I will actively be contributing inspiration, tips, and art to the group as well!

Also, If you want a bit more help with your character creation, email AnxietyConqueress@gmail.com to grab a character creation template to kick-start your quest to a healthy fear-free relationship.

Happy playing!

# About the Author

Lover of all things fantasy, magical, and nerdy, author of *Damsel No More!* Emily Davis applies the fun strategies of role-play gaming to the life-coaching world. After surviving years of relationship abuse, she made it her quest to help women slay their fears and create healthy relationships through play. Emily and her family, including dog and bunnies, adventure from Lake Tahoe, California, where she finds inspiration for her clients, art, and writing in the beauty of the mountains. To check out more of Emily's work visit her website, damselnomore.com.

CPSIA information can be obtained
at www.ICGtesting.com
Printed in the USA
JSHW021542220920
8145JS00001B/15